INTERNET INFERNO

INTERNET INFERNO

*A Contemporary Warning and Reminder
Regarding this Ancient Truth –
"The Tongue is a Fire,
the Very World of Iniquity,
and is Set on Fire
by Hell"
James 3:6*

Published by:

The Armoury Ministries

www.thearmouryministries.org

Unless otherwise indicated, all Scripture references are taken from the New American Standard Bible, Copyright © 1960, 1962, 1963, 1968, 1971, 1972, 1973, 1975, 1977, 1995 by The Lockman Foundation

Internet Inferno: A Contemporary Warning and Reminder Regarding this Ancient Truth - "The Tongue is a Fire, the Very World of Iniquity, and is Set on Fire by Hell" James 3:6

ISBN: 978-1-935358-15-2
Copyright © 2017 by Michael John Beasley. Library of Congress Cataloging-in-Publication Data Michael John Beasley

Internet Inferno: Library of Congress Registration Claim: [Claim pending: 1-5938423501]

All rights reserved. No part of this book may be reproduced, stored in a retrieval system, or transmitted in any form or by any means – electronic, mechanical, photocopy, recording, or otherwise – without permission of the publisher, except for brief quotations in printed reviews.

Fire vector image on cover and chapter divisions created by Freepik: www.freepik.com.

For more information go to: www.thearmouryministries.org

To Sandra

Leviticus 19:16–18

: 16 'You shall not go about as a slanderer among your people, and
you are not to act against the life of your neighbor;
I am the LORD.
17 'You shall not hate your fellow countryman in your heart; you may
surely reprove your neighbor,
but shall not incur sin because of him.
18 'You shall not take vengeance, nor bear any grudge
against the sons of your people,
but you shall love your neighbor as yourself;
I am the LORD."

INTERNET INFERNO

TABLE OF CONTENTS

PREFACE: JAMES 3:6 - A TIMELESS WARNING FOR ALL - 9

CHAPTER 1: A TALE OF INESTIMABLE EVIL - 15

CHAPTER 2: A VIRTUAL HELL ON EARTH - 27

CHAPTER 3: YOU SHALL NOT HATE YOUR NEIGHBOR - 39

CHAPTER 4: THE PERILS OF SATANIC IMITATION - 53

CHAPTER 5: YOU *SHALL* REBUKE YOUR NEIGHBOR - 65

CHAPTER 6: THE SWORD VS. THE FLAME-THROWER - 75

CONCLUSION: THE MOST SLANDERED PERSON IN HISTORY - 89

APPENDIX I: THE DESPICABLE EXAMPLE OF MR. TALKATIVE - 101

APPENDIX II: MATTHEW HENRY ON LEVITICUS 19:11-18 - 115

INTERNET INFERNO

~ PREFACE ~
JAMES 3:6 - A TIMELESS WARNING FOR ALL

As is the case with any book, I cannot know in advance who will eventually read this material. Especially in light of the breadth of our topic at hand, many different individuals from different backgrounds may be inclined to examine the contents of this volume. With this in mind, I do hope to write this appeal to a fairly broad audience. *First*, as a Christian and a pastor, I have written this book as an exhortation to fellow Christians. I am greatly concerned about the manner in which electronic communication, when poorly utilized, can serve to dishonor the Gospel and the reputation of the church. *Second*, I have also written this book with the non-Christian in mind. Sadly, too much of what is published on the Internet today, in the name of Christ, has little to do with Christ at all. Because of this, there are many instances in which the Gospel is confused or significantly obfuscated. Situations like these require scriptural clarity, and it is my hope and prayer to offer some measure of clarity within this title. Of course, some non-Christians reading this book will actually be *false-Christians*, that is, individuals who think that they are a Christian but are instead self-deceived. Such self-deception is dangerous and requires an honest and open rebuke, much like what was given to John Bunyan's character *Talkative* in his classic work *The Pilgrim's Progress*. When Christian's companion, Faithful, reproved Talkative for his many inconsistencies of life and doctrine, the dialogue ended with Talkative's abrupt departure from their midst. When this happened, Christian said to Faithful:

> "You did well to talk so plainly to him as you did. There is but little of this faithful dealing with men now-a-days, and that makes religion to stink so in the nostrils of many as it doth; for they are these talkative fools, whose religion is only in word, and who are debauched and vain in their conversation, that (being so much admitted into the fellowship of the godly) do puzzle the world, blemish Christianity, and grieve the sincere. I wish that all men would deal with such as you have done; then should they either be made more conformable to religion, or the company of saints would be too hot for them."

Bunyan understood a crucial principle that our own generation desperately needs to rediscover: The lack of godly reproof (Matthew 18:15-18, Leviticus 19:16-19) in the modern church creates a ripe environment for men like Talkative, whose conduct does "puzzle the world, blemish Christianity...grieve the sincere" and "makes religion to stink." Moreover, failure to expose and rebuke such hypocrisy is both an act of indifference and sinful complicity:

> James 4:17: Therefore, to one who knows the right thing to do, and does not do it, to him it is sin.

Whenever there is a genuine need to issue a word of correction to others, it is imperative that such a correction be given with genuine wisdom and love. When we fail to do this, we enter into a dangerous hypocrisy which begets more harm than good. Today, our technologically oriented society has been equipped with powerful tools which magnify one's public influence, for better or for worse; and too often these tools are used recklessly and with little self-examination. Like a child that is handed a loaded gun, our society has precious little comprehension of the destruction that can be wielded through the wicked use of online media. In view of this, the simple contention of this work is as follows: The use of electronic communication today (principally *via* the Internet) often constitutes a cesspool of evil speech, the likes of which regularly violate the ancient warnings of James:

> James 3:5-8: 5 ...the tongue is a small part of the body, and yet it boasts of great things. See how great a forest is set aflame by such a small fire! *6 And the tongue is a fire, the very world of iniquity; the tongue is set among our members as that which defiles the entire body, and sets on fire the course of our life, and is set on fire by hell.* 7 For every species of beasts and birds, of reptiles and creatures of

A TIMELESS WARNING FOR ALL

> the sea, is tamed and has been tamed by the human race. 8 But no one can tame the tongue; it is a restless evil and full of deadly poison. (italics mine)

In this text, James reminds us of the *hellish* nature of the tongue,[1] and, by extension, any communication that flows from mere mortals. This is the very basis of thought behind this book's title, *Internet Inferno*. The word *inferno* is derived from the Latin term *infernus*, which simply means *hell*.[2] It is my unrelenting argument within these pages that much of what takes place on the worldwide web is, in fact, *hellish*. As soon as I say this, I'm quite sure that the Internet's multiple problems may come to your mind: pornography and marketing scams, for example. Others have written on these grave problems and so I will defer to their works. However, in

---

[1] "'And it is set on fire of hell.' Observe hence, Hell has more to do in promoting of fire of the tongue than men are generally aware of. It is from some diabolical designs, that men's tongues are inflamed. The devil is expressly called a liar, a murderer, an accuser of the brethren; and, whenever men's tongues are employed in any of these ways, they are set on fire of hell. The Holy Ghost indeed once descended in cloven tongues as of fire, Acts 2. And, where the tongue is thus guided and wrought upon by a fire from heaven, there it kindleth good thoughts, holy affections, and ardent devotions. But when it is set on fire of hell, as in all undue heats it is, there it is mischievous, producing rage and hatred, and those things which serve the purposes of the devil. As therefore you would dread fires and flames, you should dread contentions, revilings, slanders, lies, and every thing that would kindle the fire of wrath in your own spirit or in the spirits of others." Matthew Henry, Matthew Henry's Commentary on the Whole Bible: Complete and Unabridged in One Volume (Peabody: Hendrickson, 1994), 2414.

[2] (ɪnˈfɜːnəʊ) [It. inferno:—late L. infernus hell (Ambrose).] Hell; a place of torment or misery compared to hell; a place likened in some respect to the Inferno of Dante's Divine Comedy. (Oxford English Dictionary Second Edition on CD-ROM (v. 4.0) © Oxford University Press 2009, Inferno)

this book I will be addressing the manner in which the Internet has become a dangerous megaphone for one of mankind's greatest and deeply underestimated forms of evil: the tongue. Whether you are a Christian or not, James' warning concerning the tongue is necessary for all. May our examination of this subject reveal our desperate need for wisdom, mercy and grace, knowing that all have sinned and fall short of the glory of God.[3]

---

[3] Romans 3:23.

INTERNET INFERNO

~ CHAPTER 1 ~
A TALE OF INESTIMABLE EVIL

The next time you take a penny out of your pocket I would encourage the reader to remember the following: Based upon Einstein's mass-energy equivalence of $E=mc^2$, the total nuclear-energy potential of that single penny is equivalent to 53.7 kilotons of dynamite, *or 1.5 times the collective power of the bombs dropped on Hiroshima and Nagasaki, in which 150,000 – 230,000 people perished.*

Just let that thought settle in your mind for a moment.

A TALE OF INESTIMABLE EVIL

Within this introductory thought-experiment resides a very important consideration. Like the penny in one's pocket, there are countless things in life that we grossly underestimate on a regular basis, whether by naiveté or indifference (or both). Yet, as the reader is already aware, the subject matter of this book is not about pennies or quantum physics; it is about the destructive potential that exists in our communication with others, particularly *within the Internet.* Of course, the Internet itself is not the problem; it is only a vehicle that can be used for good or evil. Ultimately, the central focus of this book is rooted in an ancient biblical text in which its author, James, sought to awaken his audience from their gross underestimation of the potential destructive power of yet another small object, *the tongue*:

> James 3:5–6: 5 …the tongue is a small part of the body, and yet it boasts of great things. See how great a forest is set aflame by such a small fire! 6 And the tongue is a fire, the very world of iniquity; the tongue is set among our members as that which defiles the entire body, and sets on fire the course of our life, and is set on fire by hell.

The language which James employs in this text is quite stunning when carefully considered. A forest fire is one thing, but his mention of the fires of hell points to a destructive potential that is, humanly speaking, *inestimable.* Even the destructive capacity of a penny pales in comparison with the destructive potential of a tongue that is guided and energized by the eternal abode of the damned. Additionally, when James says "…the tongue is a fire…and is set on fire by hell," he is not exaggerating for dramatic effect. Rather than being hyperbolic in his description of the tongue's destructive potential, James' grave warning brings to mind the ancient and evil co-belligerence between mankind and the Devil. It is this very co-belligerence of which Christ spoke when confronting His detractors in John 8:44:

> John 8:44–45: 44 "You are of your father the devil, and you want to do the desires of your father. He was a murderer from the beginning, and does not stand in the truth because there is no truth in him. Whenever he speaks a lie, he speaks from his own nature, for he is a liar and the father of lies."

Contextually speaking, Jesus issued this rebuke to those who had falsely accused Him in multiple ways. Christ's simple yet penetrating response reminded them that they were engaging in the same activities one would expect from the devil's own children:[4] Thus, they were lying after the pattern of "the father of lies," for whom the very fires of hell have been prepared.[5] When Jesus issued this rebuke, he was not saying that his accusers were the passive and helpless victims of the Devil. No, He was pointing out the fact that they were engaging in a willful act as the co-belligerents of Satan Himself: "…you want to do the desires of your father." Like the text in James, this is not hyperbole. It calls to mind the fact that the world in which we live is energized by two cooperative sources of evil: the evil of men and the evil of Satan.[6] When we see the manifestation

---

[4] 1 John 3:10: By this the children of God and the children of the devil are obvious: anyone who does not practice righteousness is not of God, nor the one who does not love his brother.

[5] Matthew 25:41: "Then He will also say to those on His left, 'Depart from Me, accursed ones, into the eternal fire which has been prepared for the devil and his angels;"

A TALE OF INESTIMABLE EVIL

of evil in this world, we can be sure that it is the collective work of the children of wrath, along with the rulers, powers, world forces of darkness, and spiritual forces of wickedness in the heavenly places.[7] It is therefore no surprise that, in the final judgment, the Devil,[8] along with the inhabitants of this world who are his, will be cast *together* into hell:

> Revelation 20:10: And the devil who deceived them was thrown into the lake of fire and brimstone, where the beast and the false prophet are also; and they will be tormented day and night forever and ever…15: And if anyone's name was not found written in the book of life, he was thrown into the lake of fire."

Not only will God condemn the guilty for the deeds they have done, but for the words they have said:

> Revelation 22:14–15: 14 Blessed are those who wash their robes, so that they may have the right to the tree of life, and may enter by the gates into the city. 15 Outside are the dogs and the sorcerers and the immoral persons and the murderers and the idolaters, *and everyone who loves and practices lying.* [italics mine]

---

[6] Ephesians 2:1–3: 1 And you were dead in your trespasses and sins, 2 in which you formerly walked according to the course of this world, according to the prince of the power of the air, of the spirit that is now working in the sons of disobedience. 3 Among them we too all formerly lived in the lusts of our flesh, indulging the desires of the flesh and of the mind, and were by nature children of wrath, even as the rest.

[7] Ephesians 6:12: For our struggle is not against flesh and blood, but against the rulers, against the powers, against the world forces of this darkness, against the spiritual forces of wickedness in the heavenly places.

[8] Revelation 20:10: 10 And the devil who deceived them was thrown into the lake of fire and brimstone, where the beast and the false prophet are also; and they will be tormented day and night forever and ever.

INTERNET INFERNO

Those who underestimate the destructive power of the tongue do so to their own peril and should consider the words and warnings of Scripture while they still have the opportunity to do so. Not only will mankind be judged for their actions, but also for what they speak in public *and in secret*. In the end, everything said and done will fall beneath the perfect scrutiny of God Himself

> Luke 12:2–5: 2 "But there is nothing covered up that will not be revealed, and hidden that will not be known. 3 "Accordingly, whatever you have said in the dark will be heard in the light, and what you have whispered in the inner rooms will be proclaimed upon the housetops. 4 "I say to you, My friends, do not be afraid of those who kill the body and after that have no more that they can do. 5 "But I will warn you whom to fear: fear the One who, after He has killed, has authority to cast into hell; yes, I tell you, fear Him!"

All in all, how many of us open our mouths and speak with the cautionary sense of these warnings in mind? Moreover, how often do we consider these aforementioned principles and warnings when posting our thoughts, comments, and critiques on the Internet? While this work could have focused solely on the dangers of the tongue alone (the spoken word), I have chosen to address the contextual danger of the Internet for a specific reason. My contention within this volume is that, similar to our general indifference to the penny, most people see their interactions on the Internet as having little significance, requiring little accountability. Having now become a ubiquitous commodity, electronic communication is seen by many like the meaningless contribution one leaves at the cash register for the next customer's cash tally: a copper penny of little worth. However, I can assure the reader that the Internet neither diminishes the importance of our communication nor does it nullify the aforementioned warnings of Scripture. Despite this, many continue to be deceived into believing that our electronic communications somehow fall outside the scrutiny of the eternal God. The Internet, in addition to being a potential tool for good, has especially become a useful tool in the hands of the Devil whereby he entices the masses to follow him in spreading false accusations, deception, evil speech, and lies after his own pattern as "the father of lies." Like a hellish pied piper, Satan leads many down a pathway of thinking which assumes that electronic media constitutes a grand communicative-exception within God's created Universe. When people embrace this dangerous deception, they create an *electronic-communicative inferno* – an *internet inferno*. I doubt that I need to persuade the reader of the toxic nature of the commentary available on the worldwide web. Rumors, gossip, false accusations, vitriolic arguments, churlish mockery; it seems that the list is endless. But rest assured, whatever we speak or type, (as Jesus said) "there is nothing covered up that will not be revealed, and hidden that will not be known." Whether you are a Christian or not, these are deeply sobering words for our carefree internet generation.

Within the Preface, I indicated that it was my desire to appeal to *believers (Christians)* and *unbelievers (non-Christians)* throughout the pages of this book. While those introductory comments were simple enough, I believe that it would be helpful to clarify what those labels actually mean. Too often it is the case that entire conversations take place without an adequate understanding of the very terms that are used. Because of this, we should consider what the Scriptures have to say regarding these two categories of people:

The Christian - According to Scripture, the Christian is an individual who has come to believe and trust the message of the Gospel as revealed in the Scriptures:[9] a. That God is holy[10] and therefore will not tolerate any sin,[11] but will judge all sin and condemn the unrepentant to hell;[12] b. All of mankind is fallen in sin,[13] falling short of God's glory,[14] and therefore no member of the human race[15] can save him/herself – all their deeds are corrupted by sin[16] such that the wages of their sin is death[17] and eternal judgment;[18] c. The only saving hope for mankind is Jesus Christ, the eternal Son of God[19] who became a man[20] and gave His life as a

---

[9] 1 Thess. 1:9; 2:13.

[10] Isaiah 6:1-4, Revelation 4:8: 8 And the four living creatures, each one of them having six wings, are full of eyes around and within; and day and night they do not cease to say, "HOLY, HOLY, HOLY is THE LORD GOD, THE ALMIGHTY, WHO WAS AND WHO IS AND WHO IS TO COME."

[11] Psalm 5:4–5: 4 For You are not a God who takes pleasure in wickedness; No evil dwells with You. 5 The boastful shall not stand before Your eyes; You hate all who do iniquity.

[12] Matt. 25:31-46

[13] Romans 5:12: Therefore, just as through one man sin entered into the world, and death through sin, and so death spread to all men, because all sinned—

[14] Romans 3:23: for all have sinned and fall short of the glory of God,

[15] Romans 3:9-18.

[16] Isaiah 64:6: 6 For all of us have become like one who is unclean, And all our righteous deeds are like a filthy garment; And all of us wither like a leaf, And our iniquities, like the wind, take us away.

[17] Romans 6:23: For the wages of sin is death, but the free gift of God is eternal life in Christ Jesus our Lord.

[18] John 3:18, 36.

[19] John 1:1-3.

A TALE OF INESTIMABLE EVIL

saving ransom for many[21] by dying on a cross as the believer's unblemished substitute.[22] He was raised from the dead on the third day[23] and is coming again for His people to establish them, forever, in His eternal kingdom;[24] d. The one who believes in Christ is redeemed by grace, through faith and not by their works.[25] The Christian, therefore, understands that he/she has no reason to boast, except in the Lord alone;[26] e. As the redeemed of God, the Christian has a new nature[27] by the indwelling Spirit,[28] which bears fruit for God's glory. This spiritual progress will continue within the Christian amidst an ongoing battle[29] against sin.[30] Only in eternal glory will this battle of sin end in the final resurrection[31] of God's people.[32] Until that day comes, it is the calling of all believers *to be doers of God's word, not merely hearers who delude themselves* (James 1:22).

The Non-Christian – The Bible repeatedly appeals to non-Christians to look to Christ for the hope of salvation *alone*. While Scripture is filled with multiple prohibitions and commandments, it is important to understand that all of God's revelation ultimately points to the gracious yet solemn call of the Gospel of Jesus Christ.

---

[20] John 1:14: And the Word became flesh, and dwelt among us, and we saw His glory, glory as of the only begotten from the Father, full of grace and truth.

[21] Mark 10:45.

[22] 2 Corinthians 5:21: He made Him who knew no sin to be sin on our behalf, so that we might become the righteousness of God in Him.

[23] 1 Corinthians 15:1-4.

[24] Matt. 25:31-40.

[25] Ephesians 2:8-9; Gal. 2:16.

[26] 2 Corinthians 10:17.

[27] 2 Cor. 5:17, Gal. 2:20.

[28] Romans 8:12-17.

[29] Gal. 5:18-20.

[30] 1 John 1:8.

[31] Phil. 3:20-21.

[32] Phil. 1:6.

INTERNET INFERNO

Whatever the individual's background, genealogy, social status, or ethnicity may be, the Savior's appeal is for all to come to Him in faith where they will find genuine peace and rest: "Come to Me, all who are weary and heavy-laden, and I will give you rest" (Matthew 11:28). The Savior promises that those who come to Him in faith will not perish in hell, but have eternal life.[33] He also declared that, though men are the slaves of sin, they can be made free indeed by His redeeming power.[34] Without Christ's redeeming work, the non-Christian is without hope and without God in this world.[35] This is true even if the non-Christian embraces alternate religious beliefs, because only Christ is *the way, the truth, and the life* such that *no man can come to the Father except through Him.*[36]

By expanding upon these descriptions of the Christian and non-Christian, I would ask you, the reader, to consider where you stand, especially in view of our analysis of the tongue. Without some measure of introspection, it is entirely possible to read this book while failing to consider its applicability to one's own life. Such a procedure as this is an abject failure. If you have not come to a saving knowledge of Christ, my appeal to you is to continue reading this book seeing that its multiple

---

[33] John 3:16.

[34] Matthew 1:21: 21 "She will bear a Son; and you shall call His name Jesus, for He will save His people from their sins."; John 8:34–36: 34 Jesus answered them, "Truly, truly, I say to you, everyone who commits sin is the slave of sin. 35 "The slave does not remain in the house forever; the son does remain forever. 36 "So if the Son makes you free, you will be free indeed.

[35] Ephesians 2:12–13: 12 remember that you were at that time separate from Christ, excluded from the commonwealth of Israel, and strangers to the covenants of promise, having no hope and without God in the world. 13 But now in Christ Jesus you who formerly were far off have been brought near by the blood of Christ.

[36] John 14:6: 6 Jesus said to him, "I am the way, and the truth, and the life; no one comes to the Father but through Me."

scriptural appeals and warnings will direct you, again and again, to the beauty, supremacy, and glory of Christ. It is my hope and prayer for you that you will see that, in Him, you can have true peace, joy, and freedom. I also write this to the Christian in view of the church's universal need to heed the warnings and exhortations of Scripture regarding the use of the tongue. Especially in this modern era of electronic media, it behooves Christ's body to walk circumspectly amidst this age of darkness:

> Ephesians 5:15-16: Therefore be careful how you walk, not as unwise men but as wise, 16 making the most of your time, *because the days are evil.* [italics mine]

Paul's solemn warning is quite clear: as this world continues to be engulfed in the darkness of evil, believers must be more and more circumspect as to how they walk *and speak*, as Paul also says in the same chapter: *"...and there must be no filthiness and silly talk, or coarse jesting, which are not fitting, but rather giving of thanks" (Ephesians 5:4)*. Especially with respect to the Internet, which offers unbounded visibility to our words and actions, the believer can either radiate the light of God's wisdom or be dimmed by the peck-measure of worldliness. This is no small consideration.

Finally, to the reader who may be self-deceived as a claimant of Christian faith, consider Paul's earnest call to the Corinthian church:

> 2 Corinthians 13:5: Test yourselves to see if you are in the faith; examine yourselves! Or do you not recognize this about yourselves,

that Jesus Christ is in you—*unless indeed you fail the test?* [italics mine]

Generations of weak doctrine and easy-believism have created scores of individuals who would be appalled at the thought of ever "examining themselves" to see if they are genuine Christians or not. But this is a dangerous deception. Paul's admonition to the Corinthian church was not hateful, but was filled with mercy and concern, especially for those who lacked evidence of genuine fruit.[37] Who would dare stand in indifference while watching someone walk off a precipice to their own destruction? Paul, who was constrained by the love of Christ,[38] had no such indifference. Even for those who had already apostatized, he delivered them over to Satan so that they would be taught not to blaspheme.[39] In the spirit of these apostolic admonitions, may God grant you the grace of repentance in view of the scriptural warnings and teachings under review.

In the following pages, we will further examine the destructive potential of the tongue, or in the case of the Internet, *the fingers*. The medium of communication is not the issue, instead, it is the heart that is the source of all our corruption.[40]

---

[37] Matthew 7:17–18: 17 "So every good tree bears good fruit, but the bad tree bears bad fruit. 18 "A good tree cannot produce bad fruit, nor can a bad tree produce good fruit.

[38] 2 Corinthians 5:14.

[39] 1 Timothy 1:19–20: 19 ...some have rejected and suffered shipwreck in regard to their faith. 20 Among these are Hymenaeus and Alexander, whom I have handed over to Satan, so that they will be taught not to blaspheme.

A TALE OF INESTIMABLE EVIL

Overall, the principle is simple enough. Whether by tongue or the typed word, our communication with others is a window into our very heart and soul, *for better or for worse.*

---

[40] Matthew 15:18–19: 18 "But the things that proceed out of the mouth come from the heart, and those defile the man. 19 "For out of the heart come evil thoughts, murders, adulteries, fornications, thefts, false witness, slanders."

INTERNET INFERNO

~ CHAPTER 2 ~
A VIRTUAL
HELL
ON EARTH

It was July 27, 1996, and the summer Olympic Games were proceeding as planned until a pipe bomb exploded in Centennial Park, killing two and injuring 111 people. As expected, the news media was instantly stirred into a frenzy in its pursuit of the bomber. One name arose early in the news cycle: Richard Jewell, a 33 year old security guard who was initially credited for spotting the bomb and initiating an evacuation, however, he actually became the chief suspect very quickly. The reason for this shift is as follows: former associates of Jewell's called the FBI, raising concerns about his testimony and his credibility as a security guard. Based upon this testimony alone, the FBI made the once hero of this tragedy the focus of their investigation. This change in the investigation was then leaked to the media and, as a result, the Atlanta Journal Constitution, ABC News, and CNN went after the story like a pack of rabid dogs. Jewell endured a *hellish* trial by speculation, rumor, and gossip within the mainstream media as he was characterized as a failed law enforcement officer seeking morbid attention. Without much surprise, Jewell also became an object of mockery by late night comedy programs. All this unwanted media attention continued to escalate until Jewell was formally advised that he was no longer a suspect, just a few months after the media firestorm began. It would be almost nine years later that the real bomber, Eric Rudolph, would confess to the crime, but the harm done to an innocent man had already been accomplished in less than four months. Despite several settlements and libel suits with various media outlets, Jewell had difficulty restoring his name and reputation in view of the "news" that had already been disseminated about him. As Kevin Sack of The New York Times said: "[Jewell] never felt he could outrun his notoriety."[41] On August 29, 2007 Richard Jewell died at the age of 44 due to health complications, being survived by his wife and mother. The horrific media inferno which engulfed Jewell took place over two decades ago when the Internet was still growing and gaining in popularity. Today, with the mass-appeal of Google, Facebook, Twitter, along with the countless online media and news outlets,

---

[41] http://www.nytimes.com/2007/08/30/us/30jewell.html

similar "news" firestorms are prone to ignite instantly and globally with just the click of a button, creating an internet inferno capable of incalculable destruction.

The story of Richard Jewell is not just a warning for members in the news media, it is a warning to every member of the human race, especially in view of the ninth commandment: "You shall not bear false witness against your neighbor" (Exodus 20:16). It must be clearly stated and understood: the abusive treatment of Richard Jewell was not only unethical and immoral, it was *satanic*. I say this in view of our previously mentioned text of John 8:44:

> John 8:44: "You are of your father the devil [*diabolou*], and you want to do the desires of your father. He was a murderer from the beginning, and does not stand in the truth because there is no truth in him. *Whenever he speaks a lie, he speaks from his own nature, for he is a liar and the father of lies.*" [italics mine]

Christ mentions the devil's own nature in order to explain *why* it is that he lies, making it quite clear that he is not a passive victim in his actions. It is in this sense that Christ's accusers were like their "father the devil," because they had his same desire and nature within them. The devil bears his name in light of its meaning: G. *diabolou*, meaning *slanderer*. Another name often assigned to the devil is the name *Satan* [*sāṭăn*], a Hebrew word which means *adversary, enmity, or accusation.*[42] Thus, in Revelation 12:9 he is referred to as "the serpent of old

---

[42] *Enmity, accusation,* 2252b (*śitnâ*) ed. R. Laird Harris, Gleason L. Archer Jr., and Bruce K. Waltke, Theological Wordbook of the Old Testament (Chicago: Moody Press, 1999), 874.

who is called *the devil* and *Satan*, who deceives the whole world." The very next verse reveals Satan's proclivity towards slander whereby he is called "the *accuser* of the brethren."[43] This is the expected activity of Satan because, as Christ taught, "he was a murderer from the beginning...whenever he speaks a lie, he speaks from his own nature." Sadly, Satan's diabolical and murderous nature is like our own:

> Matthew 5:21–22: 21 "You have heard that the ancients were told, 'YOU SHALL NOT COMMIT MURDER' and 'Whoever commits murder shall be liable to the court.' 22 "But I say to you that everyone who is angry with his brother shall be guilty before the court; and whoever says to his brother, 'You good-for-nothing,' shall be guilty before the supreme court; and whoever says, 'You fool,' shall be guilty enough to go into the fiery hell."

When we consider the collective lessons of John 8:44 and Matthew 5:21-22 a grave and somber truth is readily seen: After the image and likeness of Satan, mankind has a natural proclivity towards lies, deception, and murder. Moreover, the murder that Christ has in mind, in Matthew 5:21-22, goes beyond the physical act itself. What He confronts is the murder that is committed within the heart wherever hatred for others can be found. This text clarifies our fallen, sinful nature. Not only are our physical acts of sin reprehensible, but the sins of our mouth and even our heart are also worthy of condemnation. Such teaching utterly destroys the dangerously false assumption that God cares about our physical sins, but winks at sinful speech and the sinful thoughts and passions behind them. Clearly, according to Christ, the very anger of

---

[43] Revelation 12:10, italics mine.

one's heart is enough to be found guilty and worthy of entering into the fiery hell. Thus, not only are men judged for their words (spoken in public or in private), they are condemned for the evil thoughts which generate such evil speech:

> Matthew 15:18–19: 18 "But the things that proceed out of the mouth come from the heart, and those defile the man. 19 "For out of the heart come evil thoughts, murders, adulteries, fornications, thefts, false witness, slanders."

Overall, *everything is seen and judged by the holy and omniscient God.* However, some may want to suggest that Jesus was only pressing His accusations against a particularly heinous group of people in these passages, such that others, *with better intentions*, might be exempt of His indictment. If this is your thought, you need to re-read the text of Matthew 5:22: "...I say to you that *everyone* who is angry with his brother shall be guilty before the court" (italics mine). I fully doubt that you, the reader, would be so vain as to suggest that you have never been angry with another person. All of us struggle with anger such that none are exempt from Christ's teaching. When Christ issued this teaching, He was rebuking the superficial religiosity of his day. As He said: "they [the religious scribes and Pharisees] do all their deeds *to be noticed by men*" (Matthew 23:5, italics mine). Such a desire to gain the approval of men, above all, meant that these religionists neither cared for God nor loved Him (John 8:42). Every generation of humanity has revealed this dangerous tendency to believe that God only evaluates our external actions, but ignores our words as well as our inner thoughts and motives.

A VIRTUAL HELL ON EARTH

Clearly, Christ refuted this dangerous error by reminding us that our motives and thoughts are equally seen by the all-seeing God. Ultimately, what Christ taught on this subject is not at all new:

> Genesis 6:5: Then the LORD saw that the wickedness of man was great on the earth, and that every intent of the thoughts of his heart was only evil continually.

We should give careful attention to this text, for it affirms and underscores Christ's teaching in Matthew 5:21-22 as it pertains to the inner thoughts and affections of man. Contextually speaking, Genesis 6:5 is given as the very premise for God's determination to destroy the entire world by means of a worldwide flood. God's justification for this judgment is essentially twofold: 1. All of mankind committed *acts* of wickedness, and 2. All men were filled with *intentions, thoughts, and affections* that were evil. Like Christ's teaching in Matthew 5:21-22, we see the consistent truth regarding God's just and holy judgment of men: It is a just judgment that is based upon their *actions* as well as their *thoughts/intentions*. Thus, the man who may pride himself as never having committed the physical act of murder must remember that, based upon his hatred for others (from his thoughts and intentions), he is still guilty before the courtroom of the all-seeing God. Genesis 6:5 offers a stunning description of our sinful human nature, especially where it says, "...*every intent of the thoughts* of his *heart* was *only evil continually.*" Let's examine the layers of this indictment:

1. "Every intent..." [H. *wekăl-yezer*]: Literally all/every [*wekăl*] intent/purpose [*yezer*]. The word *yezer* means to form or fashion

something. It is often used to speak of a potter forming a pot out of clay. As such, it speaks of the active nature of the human mind. We are continually forming and fashioning thoughts that are all tainted with the corruption of "evil" [H. *ra'*].

2. "...the thoughts..." [H. *maḥăśāḇa*]: Similar to the Hebrew word *yezer*, this term speaks of the active process of planning and devising. In some respects, this term presses the idea of organized thought or calculation[44] as we might find in the difference between the *reactive* and *pro-active* choices of *manslaughter* and *pre-meditated* murder. All such pre-meditation is equally tainted by *ra'*, evil.

3. "...the heart..." [H. *leb*]: The Hebrew term for *heart* [*leb*] is important because it spans the entirety of a person's *affections* as well as their thoughts and intentions.[45] When Jesus quoted the commandment of love in Deuteronomy 6:5 [You shall love the LORD your God with all your heart and with all your soul and with all your might] He included the word *mind* as follows: "AND YOU SHALL LOVE THE LORD YOUR GOD WITH ALL YOUR HEART, AND WITH ALL YOUR SOUL, AND WITH ALL YOUR MIND [διανοίας], AND WITH ALL YOUR STRENGTH' (Mark 12:30). The inclusion of this word is understandable when we consider the Hebraic understanding of the *heart* of man *[leḇāḇ]*, which normally encompassed the idea of one's *mind and affections*. The Greeks tended to separate these components [heart and

---

[44] "...most frequently used is that of 'planning,' 'devising.' This variation is employed in reference to both man and God, and it appears in both Qal and Piel. Israelites, for instance, are warned not to 'devise' evil against a brother (Zech 7:10). TWOT, 330.

[45] "...the totality of man's inner or immaterial nature. In biblical literature it is the most frequently used term for man's immaterial personality functions as well as the most inclusive term for them since, in the Bible, virtually every immaterial function of man is attributed to the 'heart.'" Ibid., P. 466.

mind], whereas the Hebraic concept harmonized the two.[46] Clearly, Genesis 6:5 is not just an indictment of mankind's wicked actions, but it renders an indictment of every aspect of the inner conscience: our *intentions*, *thoughts*, and *affections*; everything is tainted by the evil of indwelling sin.

Lest the reader misunderstand the lesson before us, let it be understood that Noah and his family were not spared because they were without the same corruption of sin. After the world of men was destroyed, the Lord repeated his indictment: "…the intent of man's heart is evil from his youth…" (Genesis 8:21). Ultimately, Genesis 6:5 and 8:21 teach the following truths:

1. God is holy and will not trifle with sin, even the sinful thoughts and intentions of the human heart.

2. That the corruption of sin permeates every dimension of the human heart and mind, and that none are exempt.

3. Only by God's redeeming mercy and grace can we be spared of the judgment that we deserve due to such evil.

These lessons were given at great cost and should remind us of the following: God smote the Egyptian army to demonstrate his power to the world as well as His mercy to the nation of Israel; He caused the earth to open up and destroy Korah, his men, and their households in order to display His hatred for pride and rebellion; and the Lord brought the judgment of the fiery serpents to the nation of Israel in order to rebuke the

---

[46] *H. lebāb*: Heart, understanding, mind (also used in idioms such as "to set the heart upon" meaning "to think about" or "to want"). TWOT, 1:466.

unthankful selfishness of the people – *but in no other occasion in all of human history has God completely destroyed the entire world and its inhabitants in order to teach an important lesson for generations to come.*

Genesis 6:5 is such a lesson, and only a fool would ignore it.

Be assured of this, dear reader, though we may be the great under-estimators of our own sinful *thoughts, affections, words, and actions* (and we are), *God underestimates nothing.* He misses nothing and will ignore nothing:

> Jeremiah 17:9–10: 9 "The heart is more deceitful than all else And is desperately sick; Who can understand it? 10 "I, the LORD, search the heart, I test the mind, Even to give to each man according to his ways, According to the results of his deeds."

Jeremiah's rhetorical question ("Who can understand it [the heart]?") has the simple design of showcasing this crucial answer: *No-one but the Lord can know the human heart.* This is a sobering consideration, especially since, as we have already observed, the sinful intentions and thoughts of the human heart are enough to condemn any individual. It is for this reason that the psalmist pleads with the Lord to search his heart in order to reveal any hidden and hurtful motives within him:

> Psalm 139:23–24: 23 Search me, O God, and know my heart; Try me and know my anxious thoughts; 24 And see if there be any hurtful way in me, And lead me in the everlasting way.

A VIRTUAL HELL ON EARTH

The collective implications of these truths must remind us that even the *hidden desire* to speak (or type) evil against another is seen by God and adjudicated by Him as wickedness. Thus, the person who refrains from slandering others by word or by keyboard must not boast in his *inaction*. If he is still harboring the desire for such sin in his heart, he remains guilty in view of the *hurtful ways within him*. Like an ounce of poison in a glass of water, sin saturates every aspect of human nature. This sad reality reminds us that, whether by the physical act of sin or by the transgressions of the heart, all are condemned by the holy and righteous Lord:

> Romans 3:9–18: 9 …we have already charged that both Jews and Greeks are all under sin; 10 as it is written, "THERE IS NONE RIGHTEOUS, NOT EVEN ONE; 11 THERE IS NONE WHO UNDERSTANDS, THERE IS NONE WHO SEEKS FOR GOD; 12 ALL HAVE TURNED ASIDE, TOGETHER THEY HAVE BECOME USELESS; THERE IS NONE WHO DOES GOOD, THERE IS NOT EVEN ONE." 13 "THEIR THROAT IS AN OPEN GRAVE, WITH THEIR TONGUES THEY KEEP DECEIVING," "THE POISON OF ASPS IS UNDER THEIR LIPS"; 14 "WHOSE MOUTH IS FULL OF CURSING AND BITTERNESS"; 15 "THEIR FEET ARE SWIFT TO SHED BLOOD, 16 DESTRUCTION AND MISERY ARE IN THEIR PATHS, 17 AND THE PATH OF PEACE THEY HAVE NOT KNOWN." 18 "THERE IS NO FEAR OF GOD BEFORE THEIR EYES."

Our deep underestimation of the dangers of the tongue correspond significantly with our underestimation of sinful human nature. Yet Paul ties them together by reminding us that *"their throat is an open grave; with their tongues they keep deceiving; the poison of asps is under their lips; whose mouth is full of cursing and bitterness."* Clearly, *by nature, word, and action* there is none righteous, *not even one*. All such truth about the sinful nature of *all* of mankind could lead one to despair, especially if this is all there is to say. If in the reading of these texts you feel such despair, let me strongly encourage you to go to the conclusion of this book. In that section, you will find the only remedy to this reality of sin and God's condemnation of it.

To those reading this book who make a public claim of Christian faith, please consider the warnings of these passages with great care. The next time you are tempted to issue a false or churlish word against another person on the Internet (or in any context), remember that Satan would gladly have you believe the deception that your words and thoughts are of no account. Moreover, beware of the lie which suggests that our use of the Internet changes anything. Should you be drawn into such a deception, just remember that this means you are entering into a co-belligerence with *the father of lies* against the plan and will of God. Like Satan, you are not a passive victim in this. God will deal with all mankind, not only on the basis of their *actions*, but also their also on the basis of their every *word* and *thought*.

INTERNET INFERNO

~ CHAPTER 3 ~
YOU SHALL NOT HATE YOUR NEIGHBOR

When it comes to the subject of the tongue, there is an incalculable difference between the world's "wisdom" versus God's pure wisdom from above. This is especially evident when we consider the concept of evil and hateful speech. In the modern day we often hear of *hate speech* laws being enacted in order to protect select groups of people. In fact, while this book was being completed, the California legislature passed Senate Bill No. 219 (Chapter 483) in which long-term healthcare workers are now required to use the preferred pronouns of LGBT patients or risk heavy penalties. Violations

YOU SHALL NOT HATE YOUR NEIGHBOR

to this standard, the bill states, will be treated as a violation under the "Long-Term Care, Health, Safety, and Security Act of 1973" and may include the imposition of civil penalties, potentially resulting in monetary fines and possible imprisonment. The bare implication of this new law is quite stunning: A healthcare worker *can now be imprisoned* for referring to a biological male *as a male*, or a biological female *as a female*, if the patient prefers a different identity. Not only does this belie simple science, but it constitutes a flagrant rebellion against the One who, from the beginning, "made them male and female."[47] This marks a new and disturbing era for our *land of liberty*: Citizens can now be imprisoned for simply stating a fact of nature, especially if that fact has been relabeled as hate speech.

This hyper-sensitive society[48] of ours seems quite capable of finding offenses under every rock in existence, and many are quite eager to punish those who dare to violate the codes of speech established by our new, "progressive" world. This trend is not new, but instead demonstrates what has been evident for some time: Those who claim victimhood the loudest (no matter how outrageous the claim) will end up wielding

---

[47] Matthew 19:4–6: 4 And He answered and said, "Have you not read that He who created them from the beginning MADE THEM MALE AND FEMALE, 5 and said, 'FOR THIS REASON A MAN SHALL LEAVE HIS FATHER AND MOTHER AND BE JOINED TO HIS WIFE, AND THE TWO SHALL BECOME ONE FLESH'? 6 "So they are no longer two, but one flesh. What therefore God has joined together, let no man separate."

[48] Elsewhere we find that even the fear of hate speech has led many college campuses into an ideological captivity whereby professors, invited speakers, and even college presidents are being riotously shouted into silence in the name of protecting the tender sensitivities of students.

significant power and persuasion over what others may and may not say. Though the justification of such word control is nothing more than a twisted labyrinth of poor reasoning, the root of this is simple enough to understand. The actual source of all this madness is the sin of *subjectivism*. I call subjectivism a sin because it is an epistemology which renounces the supremacy of the Creator in order to exalt the creature. As God mercifully reminds us, subjectivism is the theology of the wicked:

> Isaiah 55:7–9: 7 Let the wicked forsake his way And the unrighteous man his thoughts; And let him return to the LORD, And He will have compassion on him, And to our God, For He will abundantly pardon. 8 "For My thoughts are not your thoughts, Nor are your ways My ways," declares the LORD. 9 "For as the heavens are higher than the earth, So are My ways higher than your ways And My thoughts than your thoughts."

Only a madman would exalt himself above the Almighty God and Creator of all things. Sadly, many today walk about as mini-deities and self-authorities, demanding that others comply with their own prideful delusions and declarations. They that do this confirm the proverb which says, *"A fool does not delight in understanding, but only in revealing his own mind" (Proverbs 18:2)*. The promoters of such subjectivism would gladly re-tool Isaiah 55:7 to read: "Let the wicked *embrace* his way and the unrighteous man *herald* his own thoughts." Despite this insolence, God patiently and mercifully calls on the wicked to "forsake his way and the unrighteous man his thoughts; *and let him return to the LORD.*" Such is the great and merciful call of God to all mankind: *To "trust in*

YOU SHALL NOT HATE YOUR NEIGHBOR

the Lord with all of your heart, and do not lean on your own understanding" (Proverbs 3:5).

Amidst all of the modern discussions about what constitutes hate speech, we must recognize that the holy God is the supreme judge and arbiter of what is good or evil; loving or hateful; wise or foolish. Thus, this warning from Proverbs is both strong and needful: "There is a way which seems right to a man, but its end is the way of death" (Proverbs 14:12). Whatever our thoughts and opinions may be about what constitutes hate speech, God's thoughts and ways are infinitely higher than our own. Therefore, when it comes to this matter of adjudicating our use of the tongue, we must consider what God commands and condemns:

> Leviticus 19:16–18: *16 You shall not go about as a talebearer [slanderer] among your people*; nor shall you take a stand against the life of your neighbor: I am the LORD. 17 'You shall not hate your brother in your heart. *You shall surely rebuke your neighbor, and not bear sin because of him.* 18 You shall not take vengeance, nor bear any grudge against the children of your people, *but you shall love your neighbor as yourself: I am the LORD.* [NKJV, Italics mine]

The importance and centrality of these commandments must not be underestimated, especially in view of the commandment of love (Leviticus 19:18). Christ revealed the preeminence of this command when He joined it with the commandment of love for God (Deuteronomy 6:4-5), referring to them both as the foremost commandment (Mark

12:29–31)[49] with this added emphasis: *"On these two commandments depend the whole Law and the Prophets"* (Matthew 22:40). Christ's summation of these commandments is key; for without love for God and man, all efforts of obedience are utterly worthless. Not only does this summation help us to see the centrality and primacy of love, but it also reveals the *hateful* nature of slander. In Leviticus 19:16-18, we find only two positive commands amidst 6 prohibitions, and the relationship between them all is very important. The first positive command deals with the need to rebuke (when necessary) one's neighbor. The second positive command deals with the priority of loving one's neighbor. When we look at these in context, it is evident that when it is necessary to rebuke one's neighbor, it must be done *in love* or else we run the risk of responding to others with a *hateful heart via slander, hostility, bearing a grudge, and seeking vengeance.*[50]

---

[49] Mark 12:28–31: 28 One of the scribes came and heard them arguing, and recognizing that He had answered them well, asked Him, "What commandment is the foremost of all?" 29 Jesus answered, "The foremost is, 'HEAR, O ISRAEL! THE LORD OUR GOD IS ONE LORD; 30 AND YOU SHALL LOVE THE LORD YOUR GOD WITH ALL YOUR HEART, AND WITH ALL YOUR SOUL, AND WITH ALL YOUR MIND, AND WITH ALL YOUR STRENGTH.' 31 "The second is this, 'YOU SHALL LOVE YOUR NEIGHBOR AS YOURSELF.' There is no other commandment greater than these."

[50] "Because many, under the pretext of conscientiousness, are not only rigid censors of others, but also burst out in the open proclamation of their defects, Moses seeks to prevent this preposterous zeal, shewing how they may best restrain it, not by encouraging sin through their connivance or silence, whilst they are still far from evil-speaking. For those who labour under this disease of carping and vituperating, are wont to object that sins are nourished by silence, unless all are eager in reproving them; and hence their ardour in exclaiming against them and deriding them. But Moses points out a more useful remedy, that they should bring back wanderers into the way by private rebukes, and

YOU SHALL NOT HATE YOUR NEIGHBOR

Moreover, the failure to reprove an errant neighbor *at all* is also an act of hate, being an explicit violation of the command in Leviticus 19:17 ("...you *shall surely rebuke* your neighbor...").[51] We must also remember that an errant brother may not want to hear such a word of correction, perhaps even resisting such feedback with much effort; however, love will not allow a response of silence in a time of need. The one who withholds a needed rebuke for the sake of conflict avoidance is acting selfishly and sinfully. Overall, whether by silence or a hateful rebuke, our failure to issue *loving reproof* (where it is needed) *is sin*. Thus, "friendly reproof is a duty we owe to one another, and we ought both to give it and take it in love"[52] for *faithful are the wounds of a friend, but deceitful are the kisses of an enemy* (Prov. 27:5). Without such love, all that is left is abandonment or the hellish flames of the tongue.

It should be quite evident that the manner in which we respond to others serves as an indication of what is in our hearts. In the end, *hate speech is a very real thing*, but it is not

---

not by publishing their offences. For whosoever triumphs in the infamy of his brother, precipitates his ruin as far as in him lies; whereas a well-regulated zeal consults the welfare of one who is ruining himself. Therefore we are commanded to rebuke the wandering, and not to regard our brethren as enemies. A similar course is prescribed by Christ, "If thy brother shall trespass against thee, go and tell him his fault between thee and him alone." (Matt. 18:15.) In fine, an immoderate love of fault-finding will always be found to be arrogant and cruel."   John Calvin and Charles William Bingham, Commentaries on the Four Last Books of Moses Arranged in the Form of a Harmony, vol. 3 (Bellingham, WA: Logos Bible Software, 2010), 184–185.

[51] Matthew Henry, Matthew Henry's Commentary on the Whole Bible (Leviticus 19:17): Complete and Unabridged in One Volume (Peabody: Hendrickson, 1994), 173.

[52] Ibid.

subjectively defined by the opinions and preferences of men. Instead, it is defined by God who is the Creator of all and who therefore has authority over all. Though the destructive potential of the tongue far exceeds human estimation, God has quantified and adjudicated such evil with holy perfection *and holy hatred:*

> Proverbs 6:16–19: 16 There are six things which the LORD hates, Yes, seven which are an abomination to Him: 17 Haughty eyes, a lying tongue, And hands that shed innocent blood, 18 A heart that devises wicked plans, Feet that run rapidly to evil, 19 A false witness who utters lies, And one who spreads strife among brothers.

Of the seven things that are listed as an abomination to God (things that He hates and detests), three of them emanate from the tongue. This is a stunning repetition. We should also note that, consistent with what we learned in the previous chapter, these verses strongly emphasize the relationship between the *heart, mind, and mouth;* an emphasis which is reinforced in the broader context of Proverbs 6: "A worthless person, a wicked man, is the one who walks with a perverse mouth...who *with perversity in his heart continually devises evil*, who spreads strife" (Proverbs 6:12, 14). This should remind us that a person's silence is not necessarily an indication of piety. If the desire for evil speech remains in the heart, then nothing substantial has changed, for "even a fool, when he keeps silent, is considered wise; when he closes his lips, he is considered prudent" (Proverbs 17:28). The overall implications of these passages in Proverbs 6 are quite profound. For a generation that has heard a monolithic message regarding God's love, this truth regarding His holy hatred for sin may seem alien. Yet, the message of Proverbs 6 will provide an important understanding regarding God's lawful indictment of the tongue. We will look at the three sins of the tongue which the Lord hates, *1. Lying, 2. Bearing false witness, and 3. Spreading strife.*

1. Lying: This word (lying, H. *śeqer*), by itself, represents the broadest notion of *deception, disappointment, or falsehood*[53] and is used in various contexts to speak of idolatry (Jeremiah 10:14); false prophets (Jer. 14:14); fraudulent conduct (Psalm 35:19, 38:20); the obtaining of food or wages by deception (Prov. 20:17, 11:8); swearing falsely (Jeremiah 5:2, Leviticus 5:22); and perjury (Deuteronomy 19:18). At the heart of all this conduct is the root idea of deception: The issuance of a lie beneath a pretense of truth. What is a ubiquitous habit within mankind stands as the antithesis to God's immutable faithfulness: *Psalm 89:34: "My covenant I will not violate, nor will I alter [šăqĕr] the utterance of My lips; 1 Samuel 15:29: "...the Glory of Israel will not lie [yĕśăqer] or change His mind; for He is not a man that He should change His mind." [See also Titus 1:1–2 and Hebrews 6:18].*

2. Bearing False Witness: The text of Proverbs 6:19 speaks of the "deceptive/false [*śāqer*] witness who breaths [*p̄uăḥ*] falsehoods [*kezāḇiym*]." This category of lying is one that often has a forensic emphasis to it and is most prominently known in view of the 9th commandment: Exodus 20:16: "You shall not bear false witness against your neighbor." This particular form of lying specifically centers on an intentional effort to do injury to a neighbor. Regarding the forensic nature of this prohibition, Deuteronomy 19 further reveals God's hatred of this particular transgression:

---

[53] Francis Brown, Samuel Rolles Driver, and Charles Augustus Briggs, Enhanced Brown-Driver-Briggs Hebrew and English Lexicon (Oxford: Clarendon Press, 1977), 1055.

INTERNET INFERNO

Deuteronomy 19:15–21: 15 "A single witness shall not rise up against a man on account of any iniquity or any sin which he has committed; on the evidence of two or three witnesses a matter shall be confirmed. 16 "If a malicious witness rises up against a man to accuse him of wrongdoing, 17 then both the men who have the dispute shall stand before the LORD, before the priests and the judges who will be in office in those days. 18 "The judges shall investigate thoroughly, and if the witness is a *false witness* [ʿēḏ šeqer] and he has accused his brother falsely, 19 *then you shall do to him just as he had intended to do to his brother. Thus you shall purge the evil from among you.* 20 "The rest will hear and be afraid, and will never again do such an evil thing among you. 21 "Thus you shall not show pity: life for life, eye for eye, tooth for tooth, hand for hand, foot for foot" (italics mine). Note the standard of *lex talionis* (the law of retribution) in this text: Verse 19 clearly establishes punitive consequences for those who falsely accuse another. Modern jurisprudence is far more lenient when it comes to the discovery of a false witness. However, can one imagine a world in which the false accuser received the exact punishment which he deceptively sought against a neighbor? Such a standard as this would give any thinking individual serious pause before seeking to accuse others of any crime, especially theft, rape, and murder. Though our society often winks at the act of bearing false witness, God *hates it* as that which is worthy of an exacting judgment.

3. Spreading Strife: This final expression reveals a progression of thought within Proverbs 6:16-19: The first sin of the tongue, *lying*, represents the most generalized act of deception with no consideration of who else might be effected. The second sin, *bearing false witness*, speaks of a willful act of lying against *a neighbor*. However, this third sin of the tongue, spreading *strife* [māḏōn] among brothers, points to a broader effort to broadcast the tongue's destructive influence. Such a person as this *is a*

slanderer and seeks a larger target than just one individual. Because of this, he typically employs such destructive slander in order to achieve his end: Proverbs 16:28 "a perverse man spreads strife [*mădōn*], and a slanderer [*rāgān*] separates intimate friends" (See also Proverbs 18:8, 26:20).

All such crimes of the tongue God hates and promises to judge with everlasting retribution (1 Corinthians 6:9-10). They stand as a gross violation of His holy and perfect character and are detestable in His sight. Moreover, they openly reveal what God already sees in the heart: gross arrogance (Proverbs 28:25) and hostility towards others (Proverbs 15:18). In addition to these infractions, the Scriptures reveal a variety of related practices of the human tongue:

1. Gossip: "He who goes about as a slanderer reveals secrets, Therefore do not associate with a gossip" (Proverbs 20:19). The English word gossip refers to idle speech about the affairs of others.[54] When it is said that someone has a *big mouth*, the expression normally points to a person who has little restraint of their tongue. Such chatter can range from useless or unwholesome speech to that of destructive talebearing. This sinful habit of the tongue brings to mind the warning of Proverbs 10:19: "When there are many words, transgression is unavoidable, But he who restrains his lips is wise."

2. Deceitful Jesting: When a person hides behind humor in order to mask their true intention and meaning, this is yet another form of lying and is described as the action of a madman: "Like a madman who throws Firebrands, arrows and death, so is the man who

---

[54] Gossip: "to talk idly, mostly about other people's affairs; to go about tattling." (Oxford English Dictionary Second Edition on CD-ROM (v. 4.0) © Oxford University Press 2009, Gossip)

INTERNET INFERNO

deceives his neighbor, and says, 'Was I not joking?'" (Proverbs 26:18–19). Though many may this is a harmless procedure, it is nothing more than another form of lying.

3. Coarse Jesting: As we have already established, we all have the tendency to underestimate the importance of our communication with others. Because of this, great caution should guide our attitudes and speech according to the need of the moment,[55] lest we degrade into foolish speech and coarse jesting: "there must be no filthiness and silly talk, or coarse jesting, which are not fitting, but rather giving of thanks" (Ephesians 5:4). Too often it is the case that gratuitous[56] sarcasm and coarse jesting are employed in order

---

[55] Ephesians 4:29–31: 29 Let no unwholesome word proceed from your mouth, but only such a word as is good for edification according to the need of the moment, that it may give grace to those who hear.30 And do not grieve the Holy Spirit of God, by whom you were sealed for the day of redemption.31 Let all bitterness and wrath and anger and clamor and slander be put away from you, along with all malice..

[56] The size and scope of this subject (sarcasm, irony, and mockery) exceeds the focus of this work, especially since the most relevant passages on these topics happen to be *descriptive* rather than *prescriptive* in form. This distinction is important because not all that is historically *descriptive* is necessarily *prescriptive* in the present day (see 2 Kings 1:1-15 and Luke 9:51-56). In brief, there certainly are examples of irony (1 Corinthians 4:8-10) and sarcasm (1 Kings 18:25-29; Matthew 3:7, 23:13-33a) in the Scriptures, however no such examples are given in a gratuitous and meaningless fashion, but are instead given with a didactic purpose (1 Corinthians 4:14-20; 1 Kings 18:30-39; Matthew 23:1-12) and culminate in various prophetic indictments from the Lord, such as stern warnings (2 Corinthians 13:1-2, Matthew 23:33b-36), the promise of future judgment in Hell (Matthew 3:11-12), and even capital punishment (1 Kings 18:40). All of these *prophetic* warnings and judgments remind us of God's prerogative to mock, scorn, and judge all those who dare to plot rebellion against Him and His people (Psalm 2:2–5, Psalm 37:12–13). While these discussions are important and have their place in the broader analysis of the tongue, a careful examination of such a subject would be fairly complex, requiring a measure of time and attention that exceeds the intent of

YOU SHALL NOT HATE YOUR NEIGHBOR

to address otherwise serious matters, often leading to an abandonment of genuine wisdom and reality, after all, "fools mock at sin" (Proverbs 14:9). By such a downgrade as this, foolishness and sin will ultimately prevail.

4. Feigned Graciousness: When a person speaks kindly or graciously to others, but does so by way of pretense, this too is another form of lying: "He who hates disguises it with his lips, but he lays up deceit in his heart. When he speaks graciously, do not believe him, for there are seven abominations in his heart" (Proverbs 26:24–25). Jude warned his readers regarding the wolves who crept in unnoticed, employing the stealth of a feigned graciousness: "…they speak arrogantly, flattering people for the sake of gaining an advantage" (Jude 17).

5. Giving an Ear to Slander: Not only is the one who spreads slander called an evildoer, but the one who gives an ear to such wickedness shares the same identity and guilt: "An evildoer *listens to* wicked lips; a liar *pays attention* to a destructive tongue" (Proverbs 17:4, italics mine). Many think that it is a harmless act to listen to gossip about others. Because of this, multiple TV and Internet programs thrive on an industry of gossip that has many listeners and followers. In the eyes of God, there is no difference between the purveyors of evil speech and the consumers of it. The only way to stop the raging fire of gossip is to make sure that you are not fueling it in any way, whether by the tongue or the ear: Proverbs 26:20: "For lack of wood the fire goes out, And where there is no whisperer, contention quiets down."

---

this brief book. Instead, the principal focus of this work has centered on several *prescriptions* and *prohibitions* in Scripture dealing with the tongue. The design in this is to point *plainly* and *clearly* to the Christian's need to exercise caution when using the Internet while directing the non-Christian to the *plain* and *clear* message of the Gospel.

How crucial it is to understand this principle: "death and life are in the power of the tongue" (Proverbs 18:21). God's hatred for the sins of the tongue and ear is never diminished or changed because of one's cultural background, ethnicity, socio-economic status, gender, skin color, educational level, age, or any other *real or imagined* distinction within the human race. God shows no partiality to anyone and therefore He offers no exceptions or excuses for any sin. Hate speech is quite real, but it is solely defined by the Lord and creator of all mankind, who also created our tongues. Though we, in our own vain estimation, may not find the actions of the tongue to be corrupt and sinful, we must remember to forsake our own thoughts and ways and turn to the Lord remembering that "there is a way which seems right to a man, but its end is the way of death" (Proverbs 14:12). When we make ourselves the arbiters of what constitutes good versus evil speech, we subject ourselves and others to the opinions of *madmen*:

> Ecclesiastes 9:3: This is an evil in all that is done under the sun, that there is one fate for all men. Furthermore, the hearts of the sons of men are full of evil and insanity is in their hearts throughout their lives. Afterwards they go to the dead.

In view of our indwelling sin and imperfection, self-trust is a dangerous and deadly thing. Only in the Lord and by His true wisdom from above can we gain clarity and understanding on the subject of the tongue. As James rightly said, just before he described the sinful potential of the tongue: "we all stumble in many ways" (James 3:2). If the truth were known, we all stumble in more ways than any of us can fathom or enumerate.

YOU SHALL NOT HATE YOUR NEIGHBOR

To the Christian, let it be remembered that these are sobering truths and they must be taken very seriously such that we would consider if we are walking in love or in hate. As the Apostle John said: "We love, because He first loved us" (1 John 4:19). But what the Apostle then wrote is equally important: "If someone says, 'I love God,' and hates his brother, he is a liar..." (1 John 4:20). We must guard our hearts regularly so as to examine our motives by the very words that we are willing to speak to others.

If the reader is struggling with the high standards set forth in the Scriptures, it is important to know that God's commandments reveal our sin so that we would forsake our foolishness and embrace His wisdom. As the proverb says, *"Forsake your folly and live, and proceed in the way of understanding"* (Proverbs 9:6).

~ CHAPTER 4 ~
THE PERILS OF SATANIC IMITATION

As we peel back the layers regarding the sinful nature of the tongue, we find that those layers are quite numerous and deep. The further we go, the more we find just how much we underestimate the gravity of evil speech and the sinful heart which produces it. One such layer that requires further investigation has to do with the previously mentioned subject of *satanic co-belligerence:* A subject that is repeatedly addressed in the Scriptures, though it is largely ignored in the modern day. One significant example of such co-belligerence

THE PERILS OF SATANIC IMITATION

is found in the Gospel of John. When Jesus and His disciples had entered into the region of Caesarea Philippi, the Lord asked them this question: "Who do the people say that the Son of Man is?"[57] Various responses were given by the disciples, but Peter offered this distinguishing response: "Thou art the Christ, the Son of the living God."[58] The reason why Peter's response stood out above the others is then explained by Christ:

> Matthew 16:17: And Jesus said to him, "Blessed are you, Simon Barjona, because flesh and blood did not reveal this to you, but My Father who is in heaven."

Shortly thereafter, Christ began to explain to His disciples that He must go to Jerusalem and suffer many things, be killed, and be raised up on the third day. Peter, once again, spoke out in a distinctive manner: "God forbid it, Lord! This shall never happen to You" (Matthew 16:22). Christ's immediate response must have stunned the disciples into fearful silence when He said:

> "Get behind Me, Satan! You are a stumbling block to Me; for you are not setting your mind on God's interests, but man's" (Matthew 16:23).

Both of Peter's statements were distinctive, but for diametrically opposing reasons. His first statement was distinctive and commendable because he confessed the wisdom of God: a wisdom that was revealed to him from the

---

[57] Matthew 16:13.
[58] Matthew 16:16.

Father above. His second statement was distinctive, yet it was worthy of a strong rebuke; one which revealed Peter's momentary and unwitting co-belligerence with Satan. While this narrative unveils several important truths, we will only consider three key lessons for the sake of our study:

1. Whether you are aware of it or not, this world is engulfed in a spiritual war which rages on a daily basis. This war constitutes a battle between God's true wisdom versus the lies and deceptions of men and Satan.

2. Whether you are aware of it or not, whenever you speak, you are taking sides in this spiritual battle, for better or for worse.

3. An individual's own ignorance of this spiritual battle offers absolutely no excuse when it comes to the use of the tongue.

Of all people, the Christian should have a unique awareness of this battle, especially in relation to the potential dangers of the tongue. However, the attainment of this awareness can only come by means of a daily contest against sin. Though the believer is forgiven and redeemed by God's grace, he/she is still in the process of battling against sin on a daily basis. Thus, Peter's example stands as a reminder of this important point: In one moment a Christian can be used greatly of God; yet in another moment, he can fall hard by the sins of the tongue. Like Peter, *we all stumble in many ways (James 3:2)*. All this brings to mind the stern warnings given by James, where, in James 3:5-8, he taught that the tongue can either be harnessed for good or it can be used as an instrument that is "set on fire by hell" being "a restless evil and full of deadly poison." As an instrument, the tongue is merely giving expression to what is already in the heart.[59] But we must remember that, for the child of God, *hellish* and *poisonous* speech is no longer to be a part of their pattern of life:

> James 3:9–12: 9 With it [the tongue] we bless our Lord and Father, and with it we curse men, who have been made in the likeness of God; 10 from the same mouth come both blessing and cursing. *My brethren, these things ought not to be this way.* 11 Does a fountain send out from the same opening both fresh and bitter water? 12 Can a fig tree, my brethren, produce olives, or a vine produce figs? Nor can salt water produce fresh. [italics mine]

James expresses a strong concern regarding the appropriate conduct of the genuine believer when he writes, *my brethren, these things ought not to be this way.* The antithetical nature of James' instruction is very important. The believer's tongue is not to be a vehicle for good *and evil.* Yet, whenever cursing and evil speech pours forth from one's mouth we can be sure that worldly wisdom is being treasured in the heart. This very point constitutes the broader context of what James has to say about the tongue:

> James 3:13–18: 13 Who among you is wise and understanding? Let him show by his good behavior his deeds in the gentleness of wisdom.14 But if you have bitter jealousy and selfish ambition in your heart, do not be arrogant and so lie against the truth. 14 But if you have bitter jealousy and selfish ambition in your heart, do not be arrogant and so lie against the truth. 15 This wisdom is not that which comes down from above, but is *earthly, natural, demonic.* 16 For where jealousy and selfish ambition exist, there is disorder and every evil thing. 17 But *the wisdom from above is first pure, then*

---

[59] Matthew 15:18–19.

peaceable, gentle, reasonable, full of mercy and good fruits, unwavering, without hypocrisy. 18 And the seed whose fruit is righteousness is sown in peace by those who make peace. (italics mine)

When reading the book of James it is important to observe the manner in which he writes. From beginning to end, James initiates various arguments and then further develops them as he proceeds. Such is the case in his discussion on the importance of wisdom in relation to our conduct and speech. Like an expert artist he folds in new details, verse after verse, on his portrait of godly wisdom: An argument which began in James 1:5-7 and continues in the above verses (James 3:14-18). His cumulative instruction highly reflects that repeated lesson from O.T. wisdom literature: the heart that feasts on wisdom *will speak wisdom*, but a heart that feeds on folly will only *sputter foolishness*.[60] It is in this same sense that he reminds us why some social interactions lead to godly peace (James 3:17-18), while others lead to ungodly conflict (James 3:14-16, 4:1-12, 5:9). At the heart of this dichotomy is the question of what one treasures in the heart: either true or false wisdom. According to James, there are only two categories of wisdom: 1. Wisdom *from above* (God's wisdom), and 2. Wisdom *from this fallen, earthly realm* (that which is *earthly, natural, and demonic*). As simple of a concept as this is, it is often mutilated by the temptation to blend God's wisdom with that of the world's. Yet James offers us no such concoction, for God's *pure wisdom* has no place with that which is *demonic.* Such a blending constitutes an evil co-belligerence.

---

[60] Proverbs 15:14.

THE PERILS OF SATANIC IMITATION

This lesson from James is the same one that was presented to Peter in the sixteenth chapter of Matthew. Whenever we open our mouths and speak we are either taking sides with God and His pure wisdom, or with Satan and the demonic wisdom of this fallen world. This polarity of thought is crucial to understand, lest we enter into that damnable hypocrisy which seeks to blend God's wisdom with the lies of the devil. Those who are content with such hypocrisy are repeatedly rebuked by James throughout his epistle. In summary, he exposes the hypocrisy of blaming God and others for our own sinful lusts (James 1:13-15); the sin of resisting God's authority through pride and rebellion (James 1:19-21); the contradiction of being hearers of God's word but not doers of it (James 1:22-25); the hypocrisy of laying claim to religious piety while having an unbridled tongue (James 1:26); the evil of having an attitude of favoritism towards others (James 2:1-12); the dangers of the tongue and worldly wisdom (James 3); the sin of selfish divisions (James 4:1-10); judgmentalism (James 4:11-12); arrogant presumption (James 4:13-17); materialism (James 5:1-6); a complaining spirit (James 5:9); and the use of meaningless oaths (James 5:12). He concludes his epistle with an appeal to restore those who are caught up in such spiritually dangerous hypocrisy (James 5:19-20). Clearly, James' repeated warnings regarding hypocrisy are very serious and require careful attention.

One of the most dangerous things that an individual can do is to presume that they are immune to the dangers, temptations, and condemnations that come due to sin. When such thinking prevails in a person, a duplicitous and hypocritical life will be the result, yielding a satanic co-belligerence beneath a cloak of religion. Clearly, spiritual hypocrisy is a deadly disease that cannot be ignored. Whenever it is detected, it affords the opportunity to consider what is treasured in the heart. James' warnings are needed by Christians so that they would mortify the sin of heralding worldly wisdom along with its corrupting influences. As well, the presence of unrepentant hypocrisy stands as a warning to those who claim to have saving faith, but lack the fruit which normally attends such faith. It is this warning that reminds us of the breadth of James' expressed concern, for he clearly writes with genuine believers in mind *as well as false brethren*:

> James 2:14–17: 14 What use is it, my brethren, if someone *says he has faith* but he has no works? Can that faith save him? 15 If a brother or sister is without clothing and in need of daily food, 16 and one of you says to them, "Go in peace, be warmed and be filled," and yet you do not give them what is necessary for their body, what use is that? 17 Even so faith, if it has no works, is dead, being by itself. (italics mine)

James gives us an example of an individual whose spoken words contradict their actions. The very question which James begins with in James 2:14 (*can that [professed] faith save him?*) is then answered in the 17th verse: "even so faith, if it has no works, is dead, being by itself." Clearly, James wasn't just concerned about the sinful hypocrisy of one's deeds; he was also concerned over the sinful hypocrisy of the tongue. This particular emphasis of his is not just found in the second and third chapters of James, but it is found in every chapter he wrote: 1. In James 5:9 he prohibits the sinful act of *complaining* against others; 2. In James 4:11-12 he rebukes those who *slander* brethren whereby they act as the Lawgiver and Judge; 3. In James 3:1-12 (as already mentioned) he chastises those who hurl abusive speech and curses at others; 4. In James 2:14 (as mentioned above) he exposed the hypocrisy of the false and fruitless believer who offered nothing but shallow words to those in need; and 5. In the very first chapter, James introduced his epistle with this stunning rebuke of the grave reality of an unrelentingly hypocritical tongue:

> James 1:26: If anyone thinks himself to be religious, *and yet does not bridle his tongue* but deceives his own heart, *this man's religion is worthless.* [italics mine]

When we look at the collective messages of all these texts, it is apparent that James' concern over the hypocrisy of the tongue is remarkably broad, grave, and stark; even extending to those whose hypocrisy and satanic co-belligerence unveiled nothing but a *worthless religion.* Taken together, James 2:14 and James 1:26 clearly teach us that our *deeds* and our *words* reveal who we really are. Our every motive, thought, spoken word, and action stands as a declaration of who we serve: God or Satan. As noted earlier, the Internet itself is not the source of our communicative problems. The real problem lies within any of us whenever we are seduced into thinking that the scriptural principles of communication are somehow suspended once we begin typing on a keyboard or cell phone. The fact that we are hundreds or even thousands of miles away from the individuals with whom we are communicating *changes absolutely nothing.* If anything, it should intensify our sense of caution in communication, especially when others cannot see our facial expressions or hear our tone of voice. Of all people, the disciple of Christ should set forth an example of restraint and grace rather than bitterness and cursing. As James said: "...with it [the tongue] we curse men, who have been made in the likeness of God; from the same mouth come both blessing and cursing. My brethren, *these things ought not to be this way*" (James 3:9-10). When a person engages in evil speech against others (in whatever form), they are not only imitating Satan as the "accuser of the brethren," but they are also imitating his pride and self-exaltation as well. James alludes to this very reality in the fourth chapter of his epistle:

> James 4:11–12: 11 Do not speak against one another, brethren. He who speaks against a brother or judges his brother, speaks against the law and judges the law; but if you judge the law, you are not a doer of the law but a judge of it. 12 There is only one Lawgiver and Judge, the One who is able to save and to destroy; but who are you who judge your neighbor?

When James forbids his audience from speaking *against one another*, he is not condemning godly criticism and needful rebukes that must take place within the church.[61] Instead, he is reproving another kind of communication: destructive and slanderous speech. The principal imperative in the above text, *katalaleite*, means to speak *against* another in a destructive fashion: to revile, slander, or calumniate another.[62] Semantically speaking, this term is similar to the words *diabolou* and *sāṭăn*, (both terms were reviewed in chapter

---

[61] 2 Timothy 4:2, 1 Timothy 5:20, Titus 1:13, Romans 15:14.

[62] "to speak against, to accuse, someone," with a suggestion of the false and exaggerated:2 "to calumniate." Gerhard Kittel, Geoffrey W. Bromiley, and Gerhard Friedrich, eds., Theological Dictionary of the New Testament (Grand Rapids, MI: Eerdmans, 1964–), 3.

THE PERILS OF SATANIC IMITATION

2). The argument that James advances is this: Those who choose to *speak against* another in this manner are elevating themselves as if they were God's substitute as Lawgiver and Judge. His indictment of slander enables us to see the insidious and insane nature of such a sin. Just as one's hatred and hateful speech against another is tantamount to murder (Matthew 5:21-22), so it is that the slanderer is one who elevates himself to a level of authority that only God has:

> Deuteronomy 32:39: 'See now that I, I am He, And there is no god besides Me; It is I who put to death and give life. I have wounded and it is I who heal, And there is no one who can deliver from My hand."

God alone has the authority to kill and to give life as the lawgiver and judge, and only a fool would seek to take His place in any way, shape, or form. No one can be God's equal or serve as His substitute because no one is like Him; nor does He surrender His authority or glory to another.[63] What a profoundly rudimentary lesson it is that we should be told that we are not God's substitute in this fashion! His lesson is indeed rudimentary, but sadly needful. Whenever we slander others, we are exalting ourselves as God's substitute, and such self-exaltation is yet another form of satanic imitation:

> Isaiah 14:12–14: 12 "How you have fallen from heaven, O star of the morning, son of the dawn! You have been cut down to the earth, You who have weakened the nations! 13 "But you said in your heart, 'I will ascend to heaven; I will raise my throne above the

---

[63] Isaiah 42:8: "I am the LORD, that is My name; I will not give My glory to another, Nor My praise to graven images."

stars of God, And I will sit on the mount of assembly In the recesses of the north. 14 'I will ascend above the heights of the clouds; *I will make myself like the Most High.*'" [italics mine]

Satanic imitation can take on many different forms, but all such imitation must be mortified for the evil that it is. Whether by slanderous and murderous words, or by self-exaltation as lawgivers and judges, it doesn't take much to shift from an imitation of the heavenly Father[64] to an imitation of the prince of darkness. The warnings of James are quite strong, but they are needful for the purity of Christ's body and the advancement of God's true wisdom. Just as Peter needed to be rebuked in view of his momentary satanic co-belligerence, so too does the church require a stern warning about the dangers of the tongue and the "wisdom" that is from below. In the worst of all cases, those who habitually wag an unbridled tongue reveal that their satanic co-belligerence is neither momentary nor incidental, but instead reveals a heart that treasures demonic priorities (John 8:44, James 1:26, 3:1-16). In any context, a person's words and deeds serve as indicators of what form of wisdom they treasure and serve. Thus, we will either serve the Lord with our thoughts, words, and actions or we will serve demonic and satanic purposes, *in opposition to God.*

There is no third option or reality.

Peter's own example of sin, repentance, and progress provides a helpful model seeing that we all stumble in many ways. It is unlikely that Peter saw himself as a co-laborer of Satan when

---

[64] Ephesians 5:1.

he responded negatively to the Lord's teaching. It is most likely that Peter, out of his concern for Christ, abhorred the thought of the Savior suffering and dying at all. However, neither Peter's emotions nor human reasoning could serve as a substitute for the perfect plan and will of God. So important was this truth that Jesus issued His stern rebuke against Peter in the presence of the other disciples in order to establish this lesson *for all*. And, like those disciples of yesteryear, the modern church requires this same warning regarding the potential danger of supporting and imitating Satan and his wicked agenda. Especially when it comes to the Internet, this warning should be heralded loudly and repeatedly. And just as Peter needed his rebuke when he erred in this manner, so too do all Christians when they enter into such sin against men and God. The tendency to underestimate the sin of hatred in the heart (the murderous affection that it is), along with the sin of self-exaltation, constitutes a dangerous corruption. When we do err, we must confess our sin and acknowledge our need to pursue the wisdom that is from above rather than the world's wisdom which is earthly, natural, and *demonic*. Of all people, the Christian must be the herald of that former wisdom rather than the latter.

INTERNET INFERNO

~ CHAPTER 5 ~
YOU *SHALL* REBUKE YOUR NEIGHBOR

Up to this point we have examined multiple texts which expose the sinful proclivities of the human heart and tongue. Because of this, most of our study has focused on punitive passages which condemn evil speech. While this is good and necessary, it is not enough. God is not merely a revealer of our errors and shortcomings; He is a revealer of all truth *for He is truth.* When people think of God's commandments, they often tend to think only in negative, punitive terms, as in *"thou shalt not...",* but God's word does far more than prohibit sinful conduct:

> 2 Timothy 3:16–17: 16 All Scripture is inspired by God and profitable for teaching, for reproof, for correction, for training in righteousness; 17 so that the man of God may be adequate, equipped for every good work.

The Apostle Paul gave this description of Scripture when writing to a young pastor named Timothy. Paul warned Timothy of the difficult days that would come, but he also described God's sufficient provision in the *profitable* Scriptures for such difficult days. The *ultimate profit* of which Paul spoke is more fully described in verse 17 when he writes, *"that the man of God may be adequate, equipped for every good work."* Clearly, the *ultimate profit* of God's word is *spiritual maturity.* The relationship between verses 16 and 17 reveals that in order to achieve the maturity mentioned in verse 17 the student of Scripture must seek the profit of God's word in the manner and order described in verse 16: *teaching, reproof, correction, and training in righteousness.* Consider for a moment each stage of this spiritual maturation:

> 1. The Profit of Teaching: God's Word is profitable for *teaching,* which means that Scripture is a comprehensible revelation that clearly instructs us about the reality of God's will and His attributes;, the nature of our sin, and our ultimate need for the Savior. All that is needed pertaining to life and godliness is provided through what God has revealed[65] and it is for this reason

---

[65] 2 Peter 1:3: "...His divine power has granted to us everything pertaining to life and godliness, through the true knowledge of Him who called us by His own glory and excellence."

that we need a constant diet of God's word in order to live and walk in the pathway of God's righteous wisdom.

2. The Profit of Reproof: As we are exposed to Scripture, we continue to learn just how much we fall short of its standards. This is the very concept of reproof, where we are informed about the nature and extent of our shortcomings beneath God's standard of righteousness. Reproof is an essential stage in the process of maturation because it stops us from entering into grave error and danger. Like a traffic sign which reads "wrong way," a word of reproof/rebuke seeks to prevent us from entering into the realm of sin. Though the experience of receiving such reproof can be quite difficult and emotionally painful at times,[66] it is needful for a greater good.

3. The Profit of Correction: While reproof is essential for the process of maturation, it is not enough when left to itself. This is because reproof only tells us that we are wrong, whereas correction directs us in the way we should go. Thus, if reproof is the "wrong way" sign, then correction would be the U-turn, signaling the *correct* path to follow. Clearly, it is not enough to hear that we are *wrong* in light of our sin; rather, we need to know how our way can be made *right*.

4. Training in Righteousness: Whenever we go through the process of experiencing reproof and correction, we need to proceed in the matter of practicing and applying all that we are learning. This is the process of *training in righteousness*. When a person stumbles and falls, spiritually speaking, they learn from their mistakes and proceed in the way of righteousness. This is the overall pedagogy of

---

[66] Hebrews 12:11: All discipline for the moment seems not to be joyful, but sorrowful; yet to those who have been trained by it, afterwards it yields the peaceful fruit of righteousness.

YOU *SHALL* REBUKE YOUR NEIGHBOR

God's word: God's instructions, rebukes, and corrections have the ultimate design of training us *in His righteousness*.

This cycle of spiritual maturation is very crucial to understand. Not only does it describe the details of how a Christian is led to maturity, but it especially reveals the grace, mercy, and kindness of God Himself. God's design is that we would forsake the wrong way, not as an end, but as a means to the end of walking in His righteous wisdom. This *corrective* aspect of God's word brings to mind the text of Leviticus 19:16–18 already reviewed in the third chapter. There we observed the two positive commands which supply a *corrective* to that which is *prohibited*:

> Leviticus 19:16–18: 16 You shall not go about as a talebearer among your people; nor shall you take a stand against the life of your neighbor: I am the LORD. 17 'You shall not hate your brother in your heart. *You shall surely rebuke your neighbor*, and not bear sin because of him. 18 You shall not take vengeance, nor bear any grudge against the children of your people, *but you shall love your neighbor as yourself: I am the LORD.*

These passages remind us of our sinful human tendency to respond with a hateful heart, as manifested in one of two ways: Either by silently holding a grudge or by lambasting the offender as an act of vengeance. Neither of these responses reflects true wisdom from above since they contradict what Christ referred to as the foremost commandment of love. Clearly, the issuance of a rebuke to another is remarkably important and should never be pursued for a cheap thrill, personal entertainment, click-bait, or revenge. As already noted, the Internet is a mine-field of churlish and even cruel conduct. Rather than being mindless contributors to such madness, we must treat our interactions on the Internet with the same wisdom that is required in any communicative context. Whenever we face a real or perceived need to criticize others, we must resist the temptation of resorting to base emotion and passion. Instead, there should be at least four principles that govern our thoughts, words, and actions:

1. Addressing an Offense with Love and Wisdom: When writing to the deeply troubled and divided church at Corinth, the Apostle Paul correctively explained what love actually looks like in practical terms: "love is patient…does not act unbecomingly; it does not seek its own, is not provoked, does not take into account a wrong suffered" (1 Corinthians 13:4-5). In one sweeping statement, Paul revealed how love prevails over minor offenses and unnecessary grudges. This is similar to Peter's instruction where he said: "And above all things have fervent love for one another, for 'love will cover a multitude of sins'" (1 Peter 4:8). From these texts it is clear that, before thinking that our neighbor requires a rebuke, we ought to examine whether such a response is necessary at all. While a clear act of sin requires a corrective rebuke (Matthew 18:15), lesser offenses, in many cases, may be ignored altogether. In a society that seems to be offended at everything, this principle is especially needful: Where there is godly love, there will also be the kind of patience and forbearance which can forgive and forget lesser matters. Additionally, when we approach others with love *and genuine wisdom*, we will make sure that we are dealing with facts and not rumors or personal prejudice. If we *believe* that someone requires a rebuke, then we must seek out the facts of the matter rather than relying on careless presumption, because, *"Through presumption comes nothing but strife"* (Proverbs 13:10).

YOU *SHALL* REBUKE YOUR NEIGHBOR

2. Looking to Oneself First: When a legitimate need arises for issuing a rebuke to another, a significant moment of introspection should first take place. Without such a pause, we run the risk of issuing a pride-filled rebuke which does more damage than good, as Jesus taught: Matthew 7:3–5: 3 "And why do you look at the speck that is in your brother's eye, but do not notice the log that is in your own eye? 4 "Or how can you say to your brother, 'Let me take the speck out of your eye,' and behold, the log is in your own eye? 5 "You hypocrite, first take the log out of your own eye, and then you will see clearly to take the speck out of your brother's eye." Prideful hypocrisy is a ubiquitous disease common to all human beings, and it stands as a serious threat to spiritual maturity. When we go about finding fault with others, blind to our own shortcomings, we become contradictions to the very help we claim to offer others. Without humble introspection, we act as if we are God's substitute as Lawgiver and Judge with the result that nothing but sin is accomplished through our words and actions. It is for this reason that the Apostle Paul instructs us to seek a spirit of humility and gentleness when rebuking and correcting an errant brother: Galatians 6:1: 1 "BRETHREN, even if a man is caught in any trespass, you who are spiritual, restore such a one in a spirit of gentleness; each one looking to yourself, lest you too be tempted." Without such humble introspection, the one who seeks to assist the one in error may fall into error himself by his prideful words and actions.

3. Speaking the Truth in Love: *Truth* and *love* are often treated as adversaries within our emotion-based society today. If a person is offended by a simple presentation of *facts*, their personal sense of injury may be treated as more important than the truth itself. In such a case as this, the offended party is unwilling to face reality and resultantly expects all others to become participants in his or her personal delusion. Such accommodation is often considered to be *loving*, but it is not. Ultimately, it is nothing more than hateful deception masquerading as love: "Therefore, *laying aside falsehood*, SPEAK TRUTH, EACH ONE of you, WITH HIS NEIGHBOR, for we are members of one another" (Ephesians 4:25). Though it may seem redundant, it is necessary for fallen human beings to hear: In order to speak truth, it is also necessary to *lay aside falsehood, because truth and error cannot co-exist*. As we do this, it is essential that we are armed with actual truth and not our own opinions or specious interpretations of Scripture. Additionally, when we speak truth to others, knowing that it may be difficult for the recipient to hear, we must share it with the same design of the profitability of Scripture itself: Issuing a reproof for the sake of correction and training in righteousness. When such a word of reproof is issued on the basis of genuine love, not only is God honored but a genuine hope is established for real restoration: "He whose ear listens to the life-giving reproof will dwell among the wise" (Proverbs 15:31).

4. Speaking the Truth with Loving Restraint: In this entertainment-crazed society of ours, critical commentary is often measured by its comedic content more than anything else. Especially with respect to the Internet, many self-appointed critics are eager to post eye-catching mockery of their victims for the purpose of drawing attention to themselves. While this may garner more traffic and followers, it stands in rebellion to what Christ referred to as the foremost commandment. However, the followers of Christ are called to demonstrate godly wisdom and love in their actions and communication. Since pastors are called to be examples to the flock,[67] it is crucial that they model for others what loving restraint looks like. Thus, when faced with great opposition, the pastor is to "reprove, rebuke, exhort, with great patience and instruction"[68] with the goal of correcting those who are in error: *2*

---

[67] 1 Peter 5:3.
[68] 2 Timothy 4:1-2.

YOU *SHALL* REBUKE YOUR NEIGHBOR

Timothy 2:23–26: 23 But refuse foolish and ignorant speculations, knowing that they produce quarrels. 24 And the Lord's bond-servant must not be quarrelsome, but be kind to all, able to teach, patient when wronged, And the Lord's bond-servant must not be quarrelsome, but be kind to all, able to teach, patient when wronged, 25 with gentleness correcting those who are in opposition, if perhaps God may grant them repentance leading to the knowledge of the truth, 26 and they may come to their senses and escape from the snare of the devil, having been held captive by him to do his will.

In view of all this, the following principle is worth repeating: If someone truly deserves a word of reproof, then neither silence nor evil speech is an option. As Jesus taught: "If your brother sins, go and show him his fault in private; if he listens to you, you have won your brother" (Matthew 18:15). Matthew Henry summarizes the matter well in his commentary on Leviticus 19:16-18:

"If we apprehend that our neighbour has any way wronged us, we must not conceive a secret grudge against him, and estrange ourselves from him, speaking to him neither bad nor good, as the manner of some is, who have the art of concealing their displeasure till they have an opportunity of a full revenge (2 Sa. 13:22); but we must rather give vent to our resentments with the meekness of wisdom, endeavour to convince our brother of the injury, reason the case fairly with him, and so put an end to the disgust conceived...therefore rebuke him for his sin against God, because thou lovest him; endeavour to bring him to repentance, that his sin may be pardoned, and he may turn from it, and it may not be suffered to lie upon him... Friendly reproof is a duty we owe to one another, and we ought both to give it and take it in love. Let the righteous smite me, and it shall be a kindness, Ps. 141:5. "[69]

---

[69] Matthew Henry's Commentary on the Whole Bible, pp. 173-74.

INTERNET INFERNO

In the end, the responsibility of issuing reproof to others must never be taken lightly. Such a duty can either yield great good or great harm, depending on the wisdom or lack thereof of the person issuing such a rebuke. It is not an opportunity to showcase one's own supposed wisdom, presumed spirituality, cleverness, or wit. At its best, it is an opportunity to seek growth and sanctification within Christ's body, especially when it is approached with a humble view to oneself first (Galatians 6:1b) before addressing others (Galatians 6:1a). Such an endeavor must be prayerfully sought out in love (Ephesians 4:16), with a hatred for falsehood (Ephesians 4:25a) and a commitment to truth (Ephesians 4:25b) all while holding a high esteem for the people of God (Ephesians 4:25c). In this age of the Internet, the lack of personal contact and confrontation often serves to degrade our mindfulness of these principles, but it should not be this way. Ultimately, the issuance of reproof is no trivial task, and should give anyone serious pause before giving any form of a corrective to others. When armed with these principles, we can join Paul in this matter of destroying the fortresses of false doctrine as a means of building up those who hear us rather than destroying them.

INTERNET INFERNO

~ CHAPTER 6 ~
THE SWORD VS. THE FLAME-THROWER

Proverbs 18:21 "Death and life are in the power of the tongue."

In chapter 2 we surveyed the case of Richard Jewel and the manner in which he was exposed to the hellish flames of slander. The only real villains in that story, besides the actual bomber himself, were those who eagerly spread countless falsehoods, far and wide, thereby *killing* this man's reputation before he could receive a fair hearing in a court of law. This stands as a reminder that our society no longer waits for the legal system to make its adjudication, instead, people are now tried in the court of the media and popular opinion. When we consider the reputational slaughter that Jewell endured it should be no surprise that it happened at all, especially in light of the scriptural passages evaluated thus far. The sad truth is that fallen, sinful humanity gravitates to such verbal bloodshed with little effort at all. All that is required is a small spark of an internet rumor such that a forest fire of lies and deception will rage instantly thereafter. Though such conduct is unsurprising in general, it is especially inexcusable for those who claim to have saving faith in Christ. As James said, "My brethren, these things ought not to be this way" (James 3:10). Long before the invention of the Internet, Bishop J.C. Ryle made this related and timeless observation:

> "I believe there is far more harm done by unholy and inconsistent Christians than we are at all aware of. Such men are among Satan's best allies. They pull down by their lives what ministers build with their lips. They cause the chariot wheels of the gospel to drive heavily. They supply the children of this world with a never-ending excuse for remaining as they are. 'I cannot see the use of so much religion,' said an irreligious tradesman not long ago, 'I observe that some of my customers are always talking about the gospel and faith and election and the blessed promises and so forth, and yet these very people think nothing of cheating me of pence and halfpence when they have an opportunity. Now, if religious persons can do such things, I do not see what good there is in religion.' I grieve to be obliged to write such things, but I fear that Christ's name is too often blasphemed because of the lives of Christians. Let us take heed lest the blood of souls should be required at our hands. From murder of souls by inconsistency and loose walking, good Lord,

deliver us! Oh, for the sake of others, if for no other reason, let us strive to be holy!"[70]

One must wonder what Ryle would have to say about the raging Internet inferno of our generation, especially in regard to those "inconsistent Christians" who "cause the chariot wheels of the gospel to drive heavily." Ryle's concern for his generation is equally relevant today. Because of this, it is necessary that we examine the sad and disturbing proliferation of those who slander others *in the name of Christ: a contradictory thought if ever there was one.* Such contradictory conduct as this falls into the same realm of the fruitless "Christian" (James 2:14) whose unbridled tongue proves that his "religion is worthless" (James 1:26). What is especially disturbing about this vast online trend is that it stands as a stumbling block to the message and reputation of Christ and His Gospel. Those who witness such activity may end up assuming, falsely, that God actually promotes such wicked conduct. As we have already examined in Proverbs 6, God fiercely *hates* the *lying tongue* (Proverbs 6:17), *the false witness* (Proverbs 6:19a), and those who *spread strife among brothers* (Proverbs 6:19b). How many in our society have any sense or notion that God's judgmental wrath rests on those who invest their time and energy in devising evil and spreading strife? Let no one assume for a moment that God thinks lightly of any such sin. Moreover, it is the height of hypocrisy when the professing Christian (one who claims to serve as the Lord's representative) engages in such acts of *devising and spreading of strife.* Unfortunately, it is not uncommon to find that many

---

[70] Ryle, J. C.. Holiness (Kindle Locations 1128-1136). Heritage Bible Fellowship. Kindle Edition.

THE SWORD VS. THE FLAME THROWER

do this *while claiming to be the great champions of truth and discernment.* Sadly, the Internet has become a sprawling haven in which many so-called "Christian ministries" now thrive under the pretense and cloak of actual discernment. It is typically the case that such groups or individuals are invested in the monolithic pursuit of negative criticism of others, *but nothing more than this.* A focus such as this falls short of what actual discernment is. I say this because the English word *discernment* simply means *to separate.* This is consistent with the word's use in the O.T. and N.T. Scriptures, where discernment speaks of dividing and separating *truth and error* (H. *biyn*; G. *anakrinō*, *diakrinō*). When one thinks of this simple concept it should be quite obvious that we cannot hope to discern *error* without a proper identification of, and emphasis on, *truth.* Should this procedure become imbalanced, such that the attempt to identify error is sought *with little to no regard for truth*, then such "discernment" becomes a ruse for one's own personal agenda (Proverbs 16:27: "A worthless man digs up evil, while his words are like scorching fire."). When this happens (and it happens far too often), all that is left in the wake of such a "ministry" is deception and destruction. However, this is not the calling of a genuine believer in Christ. Instead, the example of genuine discernment that should be followed is found in that of the Apostle Paul. When writing to the church at Corinth he had the difficult task of pointing out several grave errors of theirs that were dividing and destroying the church. To do this, he sought to tear down and destroy any and all philosophies they had embraced; philosophies that stood in competition with that of God's wisdom. His *rebuke* of their error was an expression of the foremost commandment (Leviticus 19:16-

18), and the words that he gave them were rooted in *genuine discernment*:

> 2 Corinthians 10:3–8: 3 ...though we walk in the flesh, we do not war according to the flesh, 4 for the weapons of our warfare are not of the flesh, but divinely powerful for the destruction [*kathairesin*] of fortresses. 5 We are destroying [*kathairountes*] speculations and every lofty thing raised up against the knowledge of God, and we are taking every thought captive to the obedience of Christ, 6 and we are ready to punish all disobedience, whenever your obedience is complete. 7 You are looking at things as they are outwardly. If anyone is confident in himself that he is Christ's, let him consider this again within himself, that just as he is Christ's, so also are we. 8 For even if I boast somewhat further about our authority, which the Lord gave for building you up and not for destroying [*kathairesin*] you, I will not be put to shame..."

We should take special note of Paul's repeated use of the word *destruction* [*kathairesin*], both in its substantive and participial forms. The term is often used to speak of dismantling or destroying something in the context of military combat. Paul used it in Acts 13:19 in reference to the Lord's destruction of enemy nations.[71] However, in 2 Corinthians, Paul was addressing the need to engage in the *spiritual battle of truth versus error*. Thus, he described his own ministry of discernment as one that sought to destroy "speculations and every lofty thing raised up against the knowledge of God" by means of the "divinely powerful" weapons which God supplies. And what are those divinely powerful weapons? Paul expanded upon this matter elsewhere when he wrote to the church at Ephesus:

---

[71] Acts 13:19, Deuteronomy 7:1.

THE SWORD VS. THE FLAME THROWER

> Ephesians 6:12–18: 12 For our struggle is not against flesh and blood, but against the rulers, against the powers, against the world forces of this darkness, against the spiritual forces of wickedness in the heavenly places. 13 Therefore, take up the full armor of God, so that you will be able to resist in the evil day, and having done everything, to stand firm. 14 Stand firm therefore, HAVING GIRDED YOUR LOINS WITH TRUTH, and HAVING PUT ON THE BREASTPLATE OF RIGHTEOUSNESS, 15 and having shod YOUR FEET WITH THE PREPARATION OF THE GOSPEL OF PEACE; 16 in addition to all, taking up the shield of faith with which you will be able to extinguish all the flaming arrows of the evil one. 17 And take THE HELMET OF SALVATION, and the sword of the Spirit, which is the word of God. 18 With all prayer and petition pray at all times in the Spirit, and with this in view, be on the alert with all perseverance and petition for all the saints…

All of the weapons in this list are *divinely powerful* because they are, in fact, God's own provision (the armor *of God*). But as Paul repeatedly indicates, the warfare to which the Christian is called to fight is not fleshly, but spiritual. And, as he indicated in 2 Corinthians 10:3–8, it is a battle which seeks the thorough destruction and annihilation of all "speculations and every lofty thing raised up against the knowledge of God": things that can only be destroyed by means of *the sword of the Spirit, which is the word of God.* What the Apostle Paul is collectively teaching in these texts is very important: Only a person who is armed with God's armor can effectively destroy worldly speculations and worldly wisdom. Yet, there is far more to Paul's ministry of discernment than the destruction of false doctrine. To see this, we need to press on further in the text of 2 Corinthians 10, paying special attention to his final use of the word *destroy* in verse 8: "the Lord gave [our authority] for *building you up* [*oikodomēn*] and not for *destroying* [*kathairesin*] you." It is interesting that Paul, after describing his *search and destroy mission* against all erroneous philosophies and doctrines, indicated that he did not seek to destroy the people at Corinth themselves, just the false teachings that they were eagerly embracing: "...if one comes and preaches another Jesus whom we have not preached...or a different gospel which you have not accepted, you bear this beautifully" (2 Corinthians 11:4). His emphasis on *not destroying but building up* the Corinthians reveals his understanding of the potential dangers that can come when a word of reproof is necessary. If we are not careful, we may destroy and humiliate the very people we seek to help. This calls to mind the lessons gleaned from the previous chapters, especially regarding the commandment of love in Leviticus 19. If an individual requires reproof (Leviticus 19:17), the correct response is to minister a word of correction to him *in love* (Leviticus 19:18). If this is not sought out, then fleshly responses will prevail in the form of slander, hatred, hostility, bearing a grudge, and vengeance. Clearly, such a hateful response was not the design of the same Apostle who taught on the priority and nature of godly love (1 Corinthians 13). Paul's *ultimate goal* was to love the brethren in Corinth by building them up [*oikodomēn*] *in the truth*. That is to say, his core desire was to have believers further strengthened in the faith as a result of his ministry of discernment to them: a ministry that entailed both the destruction of false doctrine along with the upbuilding of the church in the truth.

When such a balanced view of discernment is lost, all that remains is a personal agenda with a religious veneer. Many

THE SWORD VS. THE FLAME THROWER

who lay claim to having a "discernment ministry" seem to have more of an agenda of finding and torching any real or perceived errorist in sight. Their words of reproof become a means of showcasing their scriptural knowledge, revealing that they are devoid of any intent to *correct and restore*.[72] In light of such an agenda, such individuals seek conflict and controversy with the hope to sustain a never ending supply of online clickbait. Rather than being an actual discernment ministry, I call such an entity a flame-thrower "ministry." In many such cases there almost seems to be a sense of glee over the real or perceived discovery of any form of doctrinal error. Some become so eager to pursue this agenda that they will create their own fake theological news in order to have an imagined opponent locked in their sights, only to be incinerated and reduced to an ash heap. In other cases, upon the discovery of genuine error, the teachers of such error are personally lambasted and derogated well beyond reason or reality. Unlike a skilled physician who carefully uses a knife to extract a tumor, many discernment-practitioners prefer the use of dynamite which obliterates both tumor and patient in one fell swoop. Unfortunately, the Internet supplies no shortage of incentives for such activity. The general fear of being associated with false teaching will regularly keep Internet surfers clicking their way through those monetized websites that have turned such fear into a cottage industry. Thus, the proprietors of these sites, in an unending bid to justify their existence, must keep a regular supply of fresh controversy on display for the masses – even if it must be invented. Such a vicious cycle as this is typically undergirded

---

[72] Proverbs 12:18.

by slander, corruption, greed, self-exaltation, along with a morbid interest in destroying others for the sake of personal gain and aggrandizement.

This is not discernment, it is damnable deception.

When we remember that the Word of God is *the sword of the Spirit*, then it isn't all that difficult to realize that Scripture is not a weapon to be twisted and utilized for our own personal, selfish, and destructive agendas. Yet, sadly, too many trample this truth under foot in their hot pursuit of online attention. Unfortunately, this problem continues to spread throughout the Internet, leading many astray in the process. Additionally, such flame-thrower "ministries" continue to thrive as evidence of God's judgment over those who desire to have their ears tickled with the falsehoods or unprofitable controversies of mere men.[73] When such individuals and groups stray from God's word far enough, they end up in the same trash-heap of which Paul warned Timothy:

> 2 Timothy 4:1–4: 1 I solemnly charge you in the presence of God and of Christ Jesus, who is to judge the living and the dead, and by His appearing and His kingdom: 2 preach the word; be ready in season and out of season; reprove, rebuke, exhort, with great patience and instruction. 3 For the time will come when they will not endure sound doctrine; but wanting to have their ears tickled, they will accumulate for themselves teachers in accordance to their own desires, 4 and will turn away their ears from the truth and will turn aside to myths.

---

[73] 2 Timothy 2:23–24: 23 But refuse foolish and ignorant speculations, knowing that they produce quarrels. 24 The Lord's bond-servant must not be quarrelsome, but be kind to all, able to teach, patient when wronged.

THE SWORD VS. THE FLAME THROWER

Some men want to feed on deception, error, and mythology, and they will *accumulate for themselves* those teachers who will gladly give them such rubbish. However, the genuine believer will refuse such things. No single individual can control or stop all such online mischief, but they can assuredly avoid such errorists and their influences. It is crucial to remember that Christ Himself must never be associated with the sinful conduct of men. The One who heralded the foremost commandment, to love God (Deuteronomy 6:4-5) and man (Leviticus 19:16-18), is the very antithesis of the hate-filled and scornful activities of sinful men. If you are a non-Christian and you have witnessed many of the evils listed in this chapter, you must steer clear of associating Christ with such conduct. Remember that the very moment when Peter's lips were used to speak against the will of God, the Savior immediately rebuked him as Satan's co-belligerent. Of course, Peter's momentary error is a reminder that all genuine Christians are imperfect people who stumble in sin, *yet they repent* and subsequently grow in greater maturity over time. Yet, those who persist in the sins of the tongue, *without repentance*, point to another stark reality: the reality of *false Christians* or *false brethren*. Of course, such individuals are non-Christians, yet their unbelief is dangerously veiled by a veneer of religion. They often pose a great danger to the church through their corrupting influences. As well, they stand as a contradiction to the testimony of the Gospel through the instability and hypocrisy of their lives. In the worst of all cases, they can become the loud proponents of false teaching, even becoming the purveyors of hostility towards anyone who opposes them. Paul mentioned such *false brethren*[74] amidst a lengthy list of significant dangers and trials that he endured in the ministry:

> 2 Corinthians 11:26: 26 I have been on frequent journeys, in dangers from rivers, dangers from robbers, dangers from my countrymen, dangers from the Gentiles, dangers in the city, dangers in the wilderness, dangers on the sea, *dangers among false brethren*; (italics mine).

Scripture reveals that there are various kinds of "false brethren": *a. Those who believe that they are Christians, but are self-deceived.*[75] *b. Those who wear the garment of religion for their own personal gain.*[76] *c. False teachers who mislead others by perverting sound doctrine.*[77] Oftentimes, false brethren will possess a variety of these traits and will be difficult to detect,[78] for they often enter the church as wolves in sheep's clothing.[79] Over time, should they be revealed for what they are, they will abandon the true church thereby revealing that they are apostates.[80] Unfortunately, the Internet

---

[74] 2 Cor. 11:26; Gal. 2:4.

[75] Matthew 7:21–23: 21 "Not everyone who says to Me, 'Lord, Lord,' will enter the kingdom of heaven, but he who does the will of My Father who is in heaven will enter. 22 "Many will say to Me on that day, 'Lord, Lord, did we not prophesy in Your name, and in Your name cast out demons, and in Your name perform many miracles?' 23 "And then I will declare to them, 'I never knew you; DEPART FROM ME, YOU WHO PRACTICE LAWLESSNESS.'

[76] Jude 11, 16.

[77] 2 Peter 2:1-3, 2 Corinthians 11.

[78] Jude 3-4.

[79] Matt 7:15-19.

[80] 1 John 2:18–19: 18 Children, it is the last hour; and just as you heard that antichrist is coming, even now many antichrists have appeared; from this we know that it is the last hour. 19 They went out from us, but they were not

THE SWORD VS. THE FLAME THROWER

is a very safe place for such individuals to hide and thrive, especially since their personal lives remain hidden from view. Yet, as we considered already, nothing is hidden from God's sight; not our hearts, intentions, thoughts, desires, nor even the words that we utter in secret, for "there is no creature hidden from His sight, but all things are open and laid bare to the eyes of Him with whom we have to do" (Hebrews 4:13). Like the character Talkative, in *The Pilgrim's Progress*, such false brethren are "talkative fools, whose religion is only in word, and who are debauched and vain in their conversation, that (being so much admitted into the fellowship of the godly) do puzzle the world, blemish Christianity, and grieve the sincere." If you have ever been grieved by the perverse online conduct of one who makes a public confession of faith in Christ, you must never confuse such activities with the One who heralded the foremost commandment of love: *to love the Lord your God with all of your heart, soul, mind, and strength and to love your neighbor as yourself.*[81] *On these two commandments depend the whole Law and the Prophets* (Matthew 22:40).

In the end, genuine Christianity is marked by humility,[82] a zeal and jealousy for God's glory,[83] true discernment,[84] and love.[85] When a believer does sin (by the tongue or otherwise),

---

really of us; for if they had been of us, they would have remained with us; but they went out, so that it would be shown that they all are not of us.

[81] Mark 12:28-31.

[82] James 4:8-10.

[83] Numbers 25:1-13.

[84] 1 Thessalonians 5:21.

[85] Galatians 5:22-23.

genuine repentance will follow. If the reader has felt the conviction of sin *via* the Scriptures cited in this book, then I would encourage you to seek out those whom you may have offended and ask for their forgiveness. If you have posted something in electronic media that in any way violates the foremost commandment of love, then confess the matter to God[86] and go to the one against whom you have spoken and seek reconciliation.[87] If you are a Christian and you presently feel such conviction of sin, then please remember that there is something of far greater worth than your online image or social media fame. Infinitely greater than all such temporal trivialities is the matchless worth of Jesus Christ as revealed in the message of the Gospel.

---

[86] 1 John 1:9: If we confess our sins, He is faithful and righteous to forgive us our sins and to cleanse us from all unrighteousness.

[87] Matthew 5:21-26.

INTERNET INFERNO

~ CONCLUSION ~
THE MOST SLANDERED PERSON IN HISTORY

As we come to the conclusion of this book, I must readily confess that there is so much more that could be said on the topic of the tongue. We have only sipped a portion from what is a very deep well. What we have partaken of in this scriptural well is admittedly bitter-sweet. The bitter experience of it is the difficult task of seeing the monstrous reality of our sin. There is simply nothing pretty about such a sight. Yet the sweetness of what we have tasted is this: Everything that we have studied in the scriptures thus far points *to a very real hope*. Even the most indicting and hardest hitting commandments that we have consulted have served as a *needful and helpful tutor*:

> Galatians 3:24: Therefore the Law has become our *tutor* to lead us to Christ, that we may be justified by faith. [italics mine]

Our cumulative study of the Scriptures has surely revealed the ugliness of our sin along with our resultant guilt before God. This is exactly what God's law does: It declares us to be guilty before the holy God. Yet the dark reality which the law exposes ultimately points us to the hope of the Gospel (the good news) of being *justified* by faith in Christ. The word *justified* speaks of a guilty party being declared *just, righteous,* or *innocent* in a courtroom. In a trial setting, when the accused party is declared innocent by the judge, they are set free without any punitive damages. Such a person has been *justified* by the authority of the judge. This is exactly what happens for everyone who places their faith and hope in Christ: They are *justified* and thereby escape the eternal judgment that they deserved due to their sin. What is so powerful and beautiful about Christ is that this very salvation and deliverance from condemnation is something that only He can accomplish. No one can get to heaven by their own good works. As we have already examined, the very intents of the thoughts of the human heart saturate everything that we think and do, which means that even our best efforts are tainted by sin:

> Isaiah 64:5-6: 5 …and shall we be saved? 6 For all of us have become like one who is unclean, and all our righteous deeds are

like a filthy garment; And all of us wither like a leaf, And our iniquities, like the wind, take us away.

Left to ourselves and our own "righteousness," we are left with one answer to Isaiah 64:5, "shall we be saved?": No. The good news is the Lord has not left us to ourselves, but has given us a Mediator who became our substitute in a remarkable way:

> 2 Corinthians 5:21: He made Him who knew no sin to be sin on our behalf, that we might become the righteousness of God in Him.

According to this brief text, the Lord Jesus Christ came into this world in order to accomplish a crucial task. He was pierced through and crushed for our iniquities *as our substitute*.[88] To say that He was made sin on our behalf is to recognize that Christ, who knew no sin, was treated as though He was guilty of our transgressions. That is, our sins were *credited* to Him while His righteousness was *credited* to all who believe in Him. We must be certain that this text is understood: Imagine a situation where you were in debt for a very large sum of money, the amount of which you could never repay in several lifetimes, and someone volunteered to pay your debt *on your behalf* in order to free you from the burden of your financial obligation. The wealth that was used to purchase your freedom *was not your own*, but it came from someone with sufficient wealth to eliminate your debt. Of course, this is just an analogy and our actual debt has nothing to do with money. The real debt that is owed is the debt of sin and guilt, and it is for this very reason that Christ died on the

---

[88] Isaiah 53:5.

cross. Such a debt could never be repaid with our sin-wrought deeds: deeds which are counted as *filthy garments* in His sight. God, who is holy, rightly demands holy perfection and He can only be satisfied by an obedience that is wholly perfect. Only Christ, *the One who knew no sin*, fulfilled this standard by His *perfect obedience* to the law.

If the truth of Christ's sinlessness seems to pose a conflict to what has been presented in this book, especially in light of all that has been said about the universal reality of sin, then consider this: Jesus Christ was more than a mere man, *He was God in human flesh*. The Apostle John makes this important truth explicitly clear at the very beginning of his Gospel:

John 1:1-4: 1 In the beginning was the Word, and the Word was with God, and the Word was God. 2 He was in the beginning with God. 3 All things came into being by Him, and apart from Him nothing came into being that has come into being. 4 In Him was life, and the life was the light of men.

The fact that John is referring to Jesus Christ in these verses is once again clarified when he also says in the same chapter: *John 1:14 "And the Word became flesh, and dwelt among us, and we beheld His glory, glory as of the only begotten from the Father, full of grace and truth."* Thus, the One who is called the Word is the only *begotten from the Father* (i.e., the Son of God). He is the one of whom John says is full of *grace* and *truth*: *John 1:17 "For the Law was given through Moses; grace and truth were realized through Jesus Christ."* As we follow along the line of John's presentation of "the Word," it is clear that this revealer of *grace* and *truth* is indeed Jesus Christ, who has come in the flesh in order to *explain* the Father in Heaven (v. 18). *What John is telling us is that Jesus Christ is the consummate revelation of God to man.* What is also clarified by John's Gospel is that Jesus Christ was a real man, after all, the Word *became flesh and dwelt among us* (John 1:14) such that John was able to see with his eyes and handle with his hands this *Word of Life.*[89] Most people will acknowledge the humanity of Jesus Christ, the Son of God, but fewer still understand the reality of His deity. Consider again John's introductory description of the Word:

> *John 1:1: In the beginning was the Word, and the Word was with God, and the Word was God.*

This short verse is comprised of three important parts. First, we learn that the Word existed[90] before the formation of the Universe (*"In the beginning was the Word..."*).[91] Then we learn that the Word was a distinct person who was with God (*"...and the Word was with God..."*). But climactically, John tells this crucial truth about the Word: *and the Word was God.* In this last statement, John tells us that the Word

---

[89] 1 John 1:1–2: 1 What was from the beginning, what we have heard, what we have seen with our eyes, what we beheld and our hands handled, concerning the Word of Life—2 and the life was manifested, and we have seen and bear witness and proclaim to you the eternal life, which was with the Father and was manifested to us—

[90] This verb *was* comes in what is called what is called the *imperfect tense*, which denotes incomplete and ongoing action.

[91] John's use of this familiar phrase from Genesis 1:1 ("In the beginning God...") reminds us that before the event of creation itself, God *was* there as the *first cause of everything*.

Himself was, by nature, all that God is by nature. That is, He Himself possesses all of the same attributes and essential nature of deity. This crucial truth is affirmed elsewhere in Scripture:

1. His Eternality (*In the beginning was the Word*): John's use of the word *was*, is what is known as an *imperfect verb* which speaks of incomplete or perpetual action. Thus, the Word *was* (existed) in perpetuity. The prophecy which foretold Christ's birth affirms the truth of His *eternality*: Micah 5:2 "But as for you, Bethlehem Ephrathah, too little to be among the clans of Judah, from you One will go forth for Me to be ruler in Israel. his goings forth are from long ago, *from the days of eternity*" (italics mine).

2. His Nature as God (*And the Word was God*): The Old Testament Scriptures once again unveil this important truth about the Son of God, who would be born of a woman: Isaiah 9:6: "For a child will be born to us, a son will be given to us; And the government will rest on His shoulders; And His name will be called Wonderful Counselor, Mighty God, Eternal Father, Prince of Peace." This is an amazing prophecy. Over 700 years before the birth of Christ, Isaiah wrote this prophecy which clearly affirms what John teaches us in John 1 – that the One who would be born as a child was Himself called Mighty God.

What John affirms in his Gospel is that the Word (who was by nature God Himself), *became flesh and dwelt among us.* As the sinless Lord and Redeemer it is evident that He is worthy of worship (John 9:35-38, 20:19; Matthew 2:7-11); He possesses the power and authority to forgive sin (Matthew 9:1-6); and He has all power and authority over life and death as the returning judge of mankind (Acts 17:30-31[92]). Jesus Christ was not merely a moral man and good teacher, He was Himself God (John 1:1), the Creator (John 1:3), who became a man (John 1:14), died on the cross as our sinless substitute, and on the third day He rose again from the grave.[93] And by His perfect sacrifice, He has provided the only way in which sinful men may be reconciled with God: "But as many as received Him, to them He gave the right to become children of God, even to those who believe in His name, who were born not of blood, nor of the will of the flesh, nor of the will of man, but of God (John 1:12–13). Though the Word came to us with grace and truth, He was sadly rejected and crucified by men: *1:10 "He was in the world, and the world was made through Him, and the world did not know Him."* His rejection and crucifixion stands as clear evidence concerning mankind's sinful corruption and need for the Savior. Before Christ was crucified, the Jewish religious leaders sought out false witnesses who would give *false testimony against Jesus in order to put Him to death* (Matthew 26:59).[94] Upon such testimony, Christ was sentenced to death as a guilty man, *though He knew no sin.* He was repeatedly mocked, beaten, whipped, spat

---

[92] Acts 17:30–31: 30 "Therefore having overlooked the times of ignorance, God is now declaring to men that all everywhere should repent, 31 because He has fixed a day in which He will judge the world in righteousness through a Man whom He has appointed, having furnished proof to all men by raising Him from the dead."

[93] John 11:25–26: 25 Jesus said to her, "I am the resurrection and the life; he who believes in Me shall live even if he dies,26 and everyone who lives and believes in Me shall never die. Do you believe this?"

[94] Matthew 26:59: Now the chief priests and the whole Council kept trying to obtain false testimony against Jesus, in order that they might put Him to death;

upon, and scorned as a criminal. A crown of thorns was forced down on His already bloody head in order to mock Him as the "king of the Jews."[95] His brutalized body was nailed to a cross and, as He hung on that cross, He endured even more abuse from the slanderous tongues of those who celebrated His pending death:

> Matthew 27:39–44: 39 And those passing by were hurling abuse at Him, wagging their heads, 40 and saying, "You who are going to destroy the temple and rebuild it in three days, save Yourself! If You are the Son of God, come down from the cross." 41 In the same way the chief priests also, along with the scribes and elders, were mocking Him, and saying, 42 "He saved others; He cannot save Himself. He is the King of Israel; let Him now come down from the cross, and we shall believe in Him. 43 "HE TRUSTS IN GOD; LET HIM DELIVER Him now, IF HE TAKES PLEASURE IN HIM; for He said, 'I am the Son of God.'" 44 And the robbers also who had been crucified with Him were casting the same insult at Him.

Though Christ was repeatedly mocked and reviled, He did not respond in like kind. As the Apostle Peter reminds us:

> 1 Peter 2:22–23: 22 [Christ] COMMITTED NO SIN, NOR WAS ANY DECEIT FOUND IN HIS MOUTH; 23 and while being reviled, He did not revile in return; while suffering, He uttered no threats, but kept entrusting Himself to Him who judges righteously;

---

[95] Matthew 27:29–30: 29 And after weaving a crown of thorns, they put it on His head, and a reed in His right hand; and they kneeled down before Him and mocked Him, saying, "Hail, King of the Jews!"30 And they spat on Him, and took the reed and began to beat Him on the head.

The Savior exercised perfect restraint while being reviled and mocked by sinful men. The fact that He was sinless (a claim that we cannot make) points to a patience and endurance that is impossible to fathom. Truly it must be said that of all who have ever been reviled and slandered in human history, Christ was the most reviled of them all, and yet He did not revile in return. Not only did Christ show forth such patience while hanging on the cross, but He also extended remarkable grace. Remember that the two criminals who were crucified with Christ mocked Him at first along with the others, that is, until one of them repented and believed:

> Luke 23:39-43: 39. One of the criminals who were hanged there was hurling abuse at Him, saying, "Are You not the Christ? Save Yourself and us!" 40. But the other answered, and rebuking him said, "Do you not even fear God, since you are under the same sentence of condemnation? 41. "And we indeed are suffering justly, for we are receiving what we deserve for our deeds; but this man has done nothing wrong." 42. And he was saying, "Jesus, remember me when You come in Your kingdom!" 43. And He said to him, "Truly I say to you, today you shall be with Me in Paradise."

Though the repentant criminal had reviled Christ beforehand, Christ lovingly and graciously extended forgiveness to Him. This criminal who repented and came to saving faith in Christ came to understand these crucial truths:

1. He understood that God was a just Judge and worthy to be feared ("Do you not even fear God?")

2. He knew that he was a miserable sinner and deserved judgment, thus he solemnly warned the other thief of this truth: "...we indeed

are suffering justly, for we are receiving what we deserve for our deeds...".

3. He believed in Christ's purity and innocence as the One who *knew no sin* ("...this man [Jesus] has done nothing wrong.")

4. He trusted Christ as the Redeemer, who alone could save his lost soul ("Jesus, remember me when You come in Your kingdom!").

Just moments before his physical demise, this criminal who placed his faith in Christ experienced a miracle. His wretched and filthy sins were placed on the innocent Savior who hung there next to him. In that moment, the believing thief was pardoned of all of his transgressions committed throughout all of his life, and he was given the sure promise of eternal life with Christ on the sole basis of Jesus' perfect innocence and righteousness. Moreover, Christ suffered much more than the torment of the nails, the cross, His crown of thorns, and the cruel mockery of others: He bore the just wrath of the Father for the sins of all who are His through faith, including the believing thief who hung there beside Him. Solely on the basis of that substitutionary sacrifice of Christ, the believing thief was delivered from the surety of an eternal torment in Hell and he was given the promise of Paradise *just moments before breathing his last breath in this world.* This is the very purpose for which Christ came into the world:

> *Mark 10:45 "For even the Son of Man did not come to be served, but to serve, and to give His life a ransom for many."*

The Son of God, Jesus Christ, came into this world as a loving gift from the Father who would be lifted up and crucified for the sins of men – so that everyone who believes in Him would not perish, but have everlasting life:

> *John 3:14-16: 14 "And as Moses lifted up the serpent in the wilderness, even so must the Son of Man be lifted up; 15 that whoever believes may in Him have eternal life. 16 "For God so loved the world, that He gave His only begotten Son, that whoever believes in Him should not perish, but have eternal life."*

Yes, the Word became flesh and dwelt among us. He was crucified as our substitute and raised on the third day[96] so that those who believe in Him may be forgiven of their sin. I invite the reader to give careful consideration to these truths. Our scriptural study of the sins of the tongue have brought us to the repeated examination of God's law and commandments. By His lawful standard we have seen that we fall short of His glory.[97] Yet by that very lawful standard we have been directed to the only hope for mankind, as previously reviewed: "Therefore the Law has become our tutor to lead us to Christ, that we may be justified by faith." (Galatians 3:24).

It is my sincere prayer and hope that you will cling to Christ in faith, and that you would make that *heartfelt confession with your mouth which results in eternal salvation:* "if you confess with your mouth Jesus as Lord, and believe in your heart that God raised Him from the dead, you shall be saved; 10 for with the heart man believes, resulting in righteousness, and with

---

[96] John chapters 19-21.
[97] Romans 3:23: 23 for all have sinned and fall short of the glory of God,

the mouth he confesses, resulting in salvation" (Romans 10:9–10).

INTERNET INFERNO

~ APPENDIX I ~
THE DESPICABLE EXAMPLE OF MR. TALKATIVE

If ever there was an allegorical work that well described the challenge of discerning the spiritual condition of professing Christians, it is John Bunyan's classic work: *The Pilgrim's Progress.*[98] Throughout this work Bunyan repeatedly employs very descriptive names which clearly label his many colorful characters, and along the way the reader further discovers why

---

[98] John Bunyan, The Pilgrim's Progress: From This World to That Which Is to Come (Oak Harbor, WA: Logos Research Systems, Inc., 1995).

THE DESPICABLE EXAMPLE OF MR. TALKATIVE

those characters merit their names. In one such occasion, relevant to our discussion about the tongue, Bunyan introduced a certain character by the name of *Talkative*. Talkative, as his name implies, *liked to talk*. When Talkative is introduced, it becomes readily apparent that he was a man in whose case *"religion hath no place in his heart, or house, or conversation; all he hath lieth in his tongue, and his religion is to make a noise therewith."* When Christian's companion, Faithful, reproved Talkative for his inconsistencies of life and doctrine, the dialogue ended with Talkative's choice to separate himself from the two men. When this happened, Christian said to Faithful:

> "You did well to talk so plainly to him as you did. There is but little of this faithful dealing with men now-a-days, and that makes religion to stink so in the nostrils of many as it doth; for they are these talkative fools, whose religion is only in word, and who are debauched and vain in their conversation, that (being so much admitted into the fellowship of the godly) do puzzle the world, blemish Christianity, and grieve the sincere. I wish that all men would deal with such as you have done; then should they either be made more conformable to religion, or the company of saints would be too hot for them."

Bunyan is quite right in this summary, as delivered through the character *Christian*. The lack of loving reproof (Leviticus 19:16-19) in the modern church "makes religion to stink." Thus, the lesson of Talkative is a needful one.

Here is Bunyan's presentation of Talkative in *The Pilgrim's Progress:*

INTERNET INFERNO

NARRATOR: Moreover, I saw in my dream, that as they went on, Faithful, as he chanced to look on one side, saw a man whose name was Talkative, walking at a distance beside them; for in this place there was room enough for them all to walk. He was a tall man, and something more comely at a distance than at hand. To this man Faithful addressed himself in this manner.

FAITH. Friend, whither away? Are you going to the heavenly country?
TALK. I am going to the same place.
FAITH. That is well; then I hope we shall have your good company?
TALK. With a very good will, will I be your companion.
FAITH. Come on, then, and let us go together, and let us spend our time in discoursing of things that are profitable.
TALK. To talk of things that are good, to me is very acceptable, with you or with any other; and I am glad that I have met with those that incline to so good a work; for, to speak the truth, there are but few who care thus to spend their time as they are in their travels, but choose much rather to be speaking of things to no profit; and this hath been a trouble to me.
FAITH. That is, indeed, a thing to be lamented; for what thing so worthy of the use of the tongue and mouth of men on earth, as are the things of the God of heaven?
TALK. I like you wonderful well, for your saying is full of conviction; and I will add, What thing is so pleasant, and what so profitable, as to talk of the things of God? What things so pleasant? that is, if a man hath any delight in things that are wonderful. For instance, if a man doth delight to talk of the

THE DESPICABLE EXAMPLE OF MR. TALKATIVE

history, or the mystery of things; or if a man doth love to talk of miracles, wonders, or signs, where shall he find things recorded so delightful, and so sweetly penned, as in the holy Scripture?

FAITH. That is true; but to be profited by such things in our talk, should be our chief design.

TALK. That's it that I said; for to talk of such things is most profitable; for by so doing a man may get knowledge of many things; as of the vanity of earthly things, and the benefit of things above. Thus in general; but more particularly, by this a man may learn the necessity of the new birth, the insufficiency of our works, the need of Christ's righteousness, etc. Besides, by this a man may learn what it is to repent, to believe, to pray, to suffer, or the like: by this, also, a man may learn what are the great promises and consolations of the Gospel, to his own comfort. Farther, by this a man may learn to refute false opinions, to vindicate the truth, and also to instruct the ignorant.

FAITH. All this is true; and glad am I to hear these things from you.

TALK. Alas! the want of this is the cause that so few understand the need of faith, and the necessity of a work of grace in their soul, in order to eternal life; but ignorantly live in the works of the law, by which a man can by no means obtain the kingdom of heaven.

FAITH. But, by your leave, heavenly knowledge of these is the gift of God; no man attaineth to them by human industry, or only by the talk of them.

TALK. All this I know very well; for a man can receive nothing, except it be given him from heaven: all is of grace, not of works. I could give you a hundred scriptures for the confirmation of this.

FAITH. Well, then, said Faithful, what is that one thing that we shall at this time found our discourse upon?

TALK. What you will. I will talk of things heavenly, or things earthly; things moral, or things evangelical; things sacred, or things profane; things past, or things to come; things foreign, or things at home; things more essential, or things circumstantial: provided that all be done to our profit.

FAITH. Now did Faithful begin to wonder; and stepping to Christian, (for he walked all this while by himself,) he said to him, but softly, What a brave companion have we got! Surely, this man will make a very excellent pilgrim.

CHR. At this Christian modestly smiled, and said, This man, with whom you are so taken, will beguile with this tongue of his, twenty of them that know him not.

FAITH. Do you know him, then?

CHR. Know him? Yes, better than he knows himself.

FAITH. Pray what is he?

CHR. His name is Talkative: he dwelleth in our town. I wonder that you should be a stranger to him, only I consider that our town is large.

FAITH. Whose son is he? And whereabout doth he dwell?

CHR. He is the son of one Say-well. He dwelt in Prating-Row; and he is known to all that are acquainted with him by the name of Talkative of Prating-Row; and, notwithstanding his fine tongue, he is but a sorry fellow.

FAITH. Well, he seems to be a very pretty man.

CHR. That is, to them that have not a thorough acquaintance with him, for he is best abroad; near home he is ugly enough. Your saying that he is a pretty man, brings to my mind what I

THE DESPICABLE EXAMPLE OF MR. TALKATIVE

have observed in the work of a painter, whose pictures show best at a distance; but very near, more unpleasing.

FAITH. But I am ready to think you do but jest, because you smiled.

CHR. God forbid that I should jest (though I smiled) in this matter, or that I should accuse any falsely. I will give you a further discovery of him. This man is for any company, and for any talk; as he talketh now with you, so will he talk when he is on the ale-bench; and the more drink he hath in his crown, the more of these things he hath in his mouth. Religion hath no place in his heart, or house, or conversation; all he hath lieth in his tongue, and his religion is to make a noise therewith.

FAITH. Say you so? Then am I in this man greatly deceived.

CHR. Deceived! you may be sure of it. Remember the proverb, "They say, and do not;" but the kingdom of God is not in word, but in power. Matt. 23:3; 1 Cor. 4:20. He talketh of prayer, of repentance, of faith, and of the new birth; but he knows but only to talk of them. I have been in his family, and have observed him both at home and abroad; and I know what I say of him is the truth. His house is as empty of religion as the white of an egg is of savor. There is there neither prayer, nor sign of repentance for sin; yea, the brute, in his kind, serves God far better than he. He is the very stain, reproach, and shame of religion to all that know him, Rom. 2:24, 25; it can hardly have a good word in all that end of the town where he dwells, through him. Thus say the common people that know him, "A saint abroad, and a devil at home." His poor family finds it so; he is such a churl, such a railer at, and so unreasonable with his servants, that they neither know how to do for or speak to him. Men that have any dealings with him say, It is better to deal with a Turk than with him, for fairer dealings they shall have at their hands. This Talkative (if it be possible) will go beyond them, defraud, beguile, and overreach them. Besides, he brings up his sons to follow his steps; and if he finds in any of them a foolish timorousness, (for so he calls the first appearance of a tender conscience,) he calls them fools and blockheads, and by no means will employ them in much, or speak to their commendation before others. For my part, I am of opinion that he has, by his wicked life, caused many to stumble and fall; and will be, if God prevents not, the ruin of many more.

FAITH. Well, my brother, I am bound to believe you, not only because you say you know him, but also because, like a Christian, you make your reports of men. For I cannot think that you speak these things of ill-will, but because it is even so as you say.

CHR. Had I known him no more than you, I might, perhaps, have thought of him as at the first you did; yea, had I received this report at their hands only that are enemies to religion, I should have thought it had been a slander-a lot that often falls from bad men's mouths upon good men's names and professions. But all these things, yea, and a great many more as bad, of my own knowledge, I can prove him guilty of. Besides, good men are ashamed of him; they can neither call him brother nor friend; the very naming of him among them makes them blush, if they know him.

FAITH. Well, I see that saying and doing are two things, and hereafter I shall better observe this distinction.

CHR. They are two things indeed, and are as diverse as are the soul and the body; for, as the body without the soul is but a dead carcass, so saying, if it be alone, is but a dead carcass also. The soul of religion is the practical part. "Pure religion and

THE DESPICABLE EXAMPLE OF MR. TALKATIVE

undefiled before God and the Father is this, to visit the fatherless and widows in their affliction, and to keep himself unspotted from the world." James 1:27; see also verses 22–26. This, Talkative is not aware of; he thinks that hearing and saying will make a good Christian; and thus he deceiveth his own soul. Hearing is but as the sowing of the seed; talking is not sufficient to prove that fruit is indeed in the heart and life. And let us assure ourselves, that at the day of doom men shall be judged according to their fruits. Matt. 13:23. It will not be said then, Did you believe? but, Were you doers, or talkers only? and accordingly shall they be judged. The end of the world is compared to our harvest, Matt. 13:30, and you know men at harvest regard nothing but fruit. Not that any thing can be accepted that is not of faith; but I speak this to show you how insignificant the profession of Talkative will be at that day.

FAITH. This brings to my mind that of Moses, by which he describeth the beast that is clean. Lev. 11; Deut. 14. He is such an one that parteth the hoof, and cheweth the cud; not that parteth the hoof only, or that cheweth the cud only. The hare cheweth the cud, but yet is unclean, because he parteth not the hoof. And this truly resembleth Talkative: he cheweth the cud, he seeketh knowledge; he cheweth upon the word, but he divideth not the hoof. He parteth not with the way of sinners; but, as the hare, he retaineth the foot of the dog or bear, and therefore he is unclean.

CHR. You have spoken, for aught I know, the true gospel sense of these texts. And I will add another thing: Paul calleth some men, yea, and those great talkers too, sounding brass, and tinkling cymbals, 1 Cor. 13:1, 3; that is, as he expounds them in another place, things without life giving sound. 1 Cor. 14:7.

Things without life; that is, without the true faith and grace of the gospel; and consequently, things that shall never be placed in the kingdom of heaven among those that are the children of life; though their sound, by their talk, be as if it were the tongue or voice of an angel.

FAITH. Well, I was not so fond of his company at first, but I am as sick of it now. What shall we do to be rid of him?

CHR. Take my advice, and do as I bid you, and you shall find that he will soon be sick of your company too, except God shall touch his heart, and turn it.

FAITH. What would you have me to do?

CHR. Why, go to him, and enter into some serious discourse about the power of religion; and ask him plainly, (when he has approved of it, for that he will,) whether this thing be set up in his heart, house, or conversation.

FAITH. Then Faithful stepped forward again, and said to Talkative, Come, what cheer? How is it now?

TALK. Thank you, well: I thought we should have had a great deal of talk by this time.

FAITH. Well, if you will, we will fall to it now; and since you left it with me to state the question, let it be this: How doth the saving grace of God discover itself when it is in the heart of man?

TALK. I perceive, then, that our talk must be about the power of things. Well, it is a very good question, and I shall be willing to answer you. And take my answer in brief, thus: First, where the grace of God is in the heart, it causeth there a great outcry against sin. Secondly-

FAITH. Nay, hold; let us consider of one at once. I think you should rather say, it shows itself by inclining the soul to abhor its sin.

THE DESPICABLE EXAMPLE OF MR. TALKATIVE

TALK. Why, what difference is there between crying out against, and abhorring of sin?

FAITH. Oh! a great deal. A man may cry out against sin, of policy; but he cannot abhor it but by virtue of a godly antipathy against it. I have heard many cry out against sin in the pulpit, who yet can abide it well enough in the heart, house, and conversation. Gen. 39:15. Joseph's mistress cried out with a loud voice, as if she had been very holy; but she would willingly, notwithstanding that, have committed uncleanness with him. Some cry out against sin, even as the mother cries out against her child in her lap, when she calleth it slut and naughty girl, and then falls to hugging and kissing it.

TALK. You lie at the catch, I perceive.

FAITH. No, not I; I am only for setting things right. But what is the second thing whereby you would prove a discovery of a work of grace in the heart?

TALK. Great knowledge of gospel mysteries.

FAITH. This sign should have been first: but, first or last, it is also false; for knowledge, great knowledge, may be obtained in the mysteries of the Gospel, and yet no work of grace in the soul. Yea, if a man have all knowledge, he may yet be nothing, and so, consequently, be no child of God. 1 Cor. 13:2. When Christ said, "Do you know all these things?" and the disciples answered, Yes, he added, "Blessed are ye if ye do them." He doth not lay the blessing in the knowing of them, but in the doing of them. For there is a knowledge that is not attended with doing: "He that knoweth his Master's will, and doeth it not." A man may know like an angel, and yet be no Christian: therefore your sign of it is not true. Indeed, to know is a thing that pleaseth talkers and boasters; but to do is that which pleaseth God. Not that the heart can be good without knowledge, for without that the heart is naught. There are, therefore, two sorts of knowledge, knowledge that resteth in the bare speculation of things, and knowledge that is accompanied with the grace of faith and love, which puts a man upon doing even the will of God from the heart: the first of these will serve the talker; but without the other, the true Christian is not content. "Give me understanding, and I shall keep thy law; yea, I shall observe it with my whole heart." Psa. 119:34.

TALK. You lie at the catch again: this is not for edification.

FAITH. Well, if you please, propound another sign how this work of grace discovereth itself where it is.

TALK. Not I, for I see we shall not agree.

FAITH. Well, if you will not, will you give me leave to do it?

TALK. You may use your liberty.

FAITH. A work of grace in the soul discovereth itself, either to him that hath it, or to standers-by.

To him that hath it, thus: It gives him conviction of sin, especially the defilement of his nature, and the sin of unbelief, for the sake of which he is sure to be damned, if he findeth not mercy at God's hand, by faith in Jesus Christ. This sight and sense of things worketh in him sorrow and shame for sin. Psa. 38:18; Jer. 31:19; John 16:8; Rom. 7:24; Mark 16:16; Gal. 2:16; Rev. 1:6. He findeth, moreover, revealed in him the Saviour of the world, and the absolute necessity of closing with him for life; at the which he findeth hungerings and thirstings after him; to which hungerings, etc., the promise is made. Now, according to the strength or weakness of his faith in his Saviour, so is his joy and peace, so is his love to holiness, so are his desires to know him more, and also to serve him in this world. But though, I say, it discovereth itself thus unto him,

THE DESPICABLE EXAMPLE OF MR. TALKATIVE

yet it is but seldom that he is able to conclude that this is a work of grace; because his corruptions now, and his abused reason, make his mind to misjudge in this matter: therefore in him that hath this work there is required a very sound judgment, before he can with steadiness conclude that this is a work of grace. John 16:9; Gal. 2:15, 16; Acts 4:12; Matt. 5:6; Rev. 21:6.

To others it is thus discovered:

1. By an experimental confession of his faith in Christ. 2. By a life answerable to that confession; to wit, a life of holiness-heart-holiness, family-holiness, (if he hath a family,) and by conversation-holiness in the world; which in the general teacheth him inwardly to abhor his sin, and himself for that, in secret; to suppress it in his family, and to promote holiness in the world: not by talk only, as a hypocrite or talkative person may do, but by a practical subjection in faith and love to the power of the word. Job 42:5, 6; Psa. 50:23; Ezek. 20:43; Matt. 5:8; John 14:15; Rom. 10:10; Ezek. 36:25; Phil. 1:27; 3:17–20. And now, sir, as to this brief description of the work of grace, and also the discovery of it, if you have aught to object, object; if not, then give me leave to propound to you a second question.

TALK. Nay, my part is not now to object, but to hear; let me, therefore, have your second question.

FAITH. It is this: Do you experience this first part of the description of it; and doth your life and conversation testify the same? Or standeth your religion in word or tongue, and not in deed and truth? Pray, if you incline to answer me in this, say no more than you know the God above will say Amen to, and also nothing but what your conscience can justify you in; for not he that commendeth himself is approved, but whom the Lord commendeth. Besides, to say I am thus and thus, when my conversation, and all my neighbors, tell me I lie, is great wickedness.

Then Talkative at first began to blush; but, recovering himself, thus he replied: You come now to experience, to conscience, and to God; and to appeal to him for justification of what is spoken. This kind of discourse I did not expect; nor am I disposed to give an answer to such questions, because I count not myself bound thereto, unless you take upon you to be a catechiser; and though you should so do, yet I may refuse to make you my judge. But I pray, will you tell me why you ask me such questions?

FAITH. Because I saw you forward to talk, and because I knew not that you had aught else but notion. Besides, to tell you all the truth, I have heard of you that you are a man whose religion lies in talk, and that your conversation gives this your mouth-profession the lie. They say you are a spot among Christians, and that religion fareth the worse for your ungodly conversation; that some have already stumbled at your wicked ways, and that more are in danger of being destroyed thereby: your religion, and an ale-house, and covetousness, and uncleanness, and swearing, and lying, and vain company-keeping, etc., will stand together. The proverb is true of you which is said of a harlot, to wit, "That she is a shame to all women:" so are you a shame to all professors.

TALK. Since you are so ready to take up reports, and to judge so rashly as you do, I cannot but conclude you are some peevish or melancholy man, not fit to be discoursed with; and so adieu.

Then up came Christian, and said to his brother, I told you how it would happen; your words and his lusts could not

THE DESPICABLE EXAMPLE OF MR. TALKATIVE

agree. He had rather leave your company than reform his life. But he is gone, as I said: let him go; the loss is no man's but his own. He has saved us the trouble of going from him; for he continuing (as I suppose he will do) as he is, would have been but a blot in our company: besides, the apostle says, "From such withdraw thyself."

FAITH. But I am glad we had this little discourse with him; it may happen that he will think of it again: however, I have dealt plainly with him, and so am clear of his blood if he perisheth.

CHR. You did well to talk so plainly to him as you did. There is but little of this faithful dealing with men now-a-days, and that makes religion to stink so in the nostrils of many as it doth; for they are these talkative fools, whose religion is only in word, and who are debauched and vain in their conversation, that (being so much admitted into the fellowship of the godly) do puzzle the world, blemish Christianity, and grieve the sincere. I wish that all men would deal with such as you have done; then should they either be made more conformable to religion, or the company of saints would be too hot for them. Then did Faithful say,

> "How Talkative at first lifts up his plumes!
> How bravely doth he speak! How he presumes
> To drive down all before him! But so soon
> As Faithful talks of heart-work, like the moon
> That's past the full, into the wane he goes;
> And so will all but he that heart-work know."

NARRATOR: Thus they went on, talking of what they had seen by the way, and so made that way easy, which would otherwise no doubt have been tedious to them, for now they went through a wilderness.

~ APPENDIX II ~
MATTHEW HENRY'S COMMENTARY ON LEVITICUS 19:11-18

Matthew Henry on Leviticus 19:11–18:

Leviticus 19:11–18: 11 'You shall not steal, nor deal falsely, nor lie to one another.12 'And you shall not swear falsely by My name, so as to profane the name of your God; I am the LORD.13 'You shall not oppress your neighbor, nor rob him. The wages of a hired man are not to remain with you all night until morning.14 'You shall not curse a deaf man, nor place a stumbling block before the blind, but you shall revere your

God; I am the LORD.15 'You shall do no injustice in judgment; you shall not be partial to the poor nor defer to the great, but you are to judge your neighbor fairly.16 'You shall not go about as a slanderer among your people, and you are not to act against the life of your neighbor; I am the LORD.17 'You shall not hate your fellow countryman in your heart; you may surely reprove your neighbor, but shall not incur sin because of him.18 'You shall not take vengeance, nor bear any grudge against the sons of your people, but you shall love your neighbor as yourself; I am the LORD.

We are taught here,

I. To be honest and true in all our dealings, v. 11. God, who has appointed every man's property by his providence, forbids by his law the invading of that appointment, either by downright theft, You shall not steal, or by fraudulent dealing, "You shall not cheat, or deal falsely." Whatever we have in the world, we must see to it that it be honestly come by, for we cannot be truly rich, nor long rich, with that which is not. The God of truth, who requires truth in the heart (Ps. 51:6), requires it also in the tongue: Neither lie one to another, either in bargaining or common converse. This is one of the laws of Christianity (Col. 3:9): Lie not one to another. Those that do not speak truth do not deserve to be told truth; those that sin by lying justly suffer by it; therefore we are forbidden to lie one to another; for, if we lie to others, we teach them to lie to us.

II. To maintain a very reverent regard to the sacred name of God (v. 12), and not to call him to be witness either, 1. To a lie: You shall not swear falsely. It is bad to tell a lie, but it is much worse to swear it. Or, 2. To a trifle, and every impertinence:

Neither shalt thou profane the name of thy God, by alienating it to any other purpose than that for which it is to be religiously used.

III. Neither to take nor keep any one's right from him, v. 13. We must not take that which is none of our own, either by fraud or robbery; nor detain that which belongs to another, particularly the wages of the hireling, let it not abide with thee all night. Let the day-labourer have his wages as soon as he has done his day's work, if he desire it. It is a great sin to deny the payment of it, nay, to defer it, to his damage, a sin that cries to heaven for vengeance, Jam. 5:4.

IV. To be particularly tender of the credit and safety of those that cannot help themselves, v. 14. 1. The credit of the deaf: Thou shalt not curse the deaf; that is, not only those that are naturally deaf, that cannot hear at all, but also those that are absent, and at present out of hearing of the curse, and so cannot show their resentment, return the affront, nor right themselves, and those that are patient, that seem as if they heard not, and are not willing to take notice of it, as David, Ps. 38:13. Do not injure any because they are unwilling, or unable, to avenge themselves, for God sees and hears, though they do not. 2. The safety of the blind we must likewise be tender of, and not put a stumbling-block before them; for this is to add affliction to the afflicted, and to make God's providence a servant to our malice. This prohibition implies a precept to help the blind, and remove stumbling-blocks out of their way. The Jewish writers, thinking it impossible that any should be so barbarous as to put a stumbling-block in the way of the blind, understood it figuratively, that it forbids giving bad counsel to those that are simple and easily imposed upon, by which they may be led to do something to their own prejudice. We ought to take heed of doing any thing which may occasion our weak brother to fall, Rom. 14:13; 1 Co. 8:9. It is added, as a preservative from these sins, but fear thou God. "Thou dost not fear the deaf and blind, they cannot right themselves; but remember it is the glory of God to help the helpless, and he will plead their cause." Note, The fear of God will restrain us from doing that which will not expose us to men's resentments.

V. Judges and all in authority are here commanded to give verdict and judgment without partiality (v. 15); whether they were constituted judges by commission or made so in a particular case by the consent of both parties, as referees or arbitrators, they must do no wrong to either side, but, to the utmost of their skill, must go according to the rules of equity, having respect purely to the merits of the cause, and not to the characters of the person. Justice must never be perverted, either, 1. In pity to the poor: Thou shalt not respect the person of the poor, Ex. 23:3. Whatever may be given to a poor man as an alms, yet let nothing be awarded him as his right but what he is legally entitled to, nor let his poverty excuse him from any just punishment for a fault. Or, 2. In veneration or fear of the mighty, in whose favour judges would be most frequently biased. The Jews say, "Judges were obliged by this law to be so impartial as not to let one of the contending parties sit while the other stood, nor permit one to say what he pleased and bid the other be short; see James 2:1–4.

VI. We are all forbidden to do any thing injurious to our neighbour's good name (v. 16), either, 1. In common conversation: Thou shalt not go up and down as a tale-bearer. It is as bad an office as a man can put himself into to be the publisher of every man's faults, divulging what was secret, aggravating crimes, and making the worst of every thing that was amiss, with design to blast and ruin men's reputation, and to sow discord among neighbours. The word used for a tale-bearer signifies a pedlar, or petty chapman, the interlopers of trade; for tale-bearers pick up ill-natured stories at one house and utter them at another, and commonly barter slanders by way of exchange. See this sin condemned, Prov. 11:13; 20:19; Jer. 9:4, 5; Eze. 22:9. Or, 2, In witness-bearing: Neither shalt thou stand as a witness against the blood of thy neighbour, if his blood be innocent, nor join in confederacy with such bloody men as those described," Prov. 1:11, 12. The Jewish doctors put this further sense upon it: "Thou shalt not stand by and see thy brother in danger, but thou shalt come in to his relief and succour, though it be with the peril of thy own life or limb;" they add, "He that can by his testimony clear one that is accused is obliged by this law to do it;" see Prov. 24:11, 12.

VII. We are commanded to rebuke our neighbour in love (v. 17): Thou shalt in any wise rebuke thy neighbour. 1. Rather rebuke him than hate him for an injury done to thyself. If we apprehend that our neighbour has any way wronged us, we must not conceive a secret grudge against him, and estrange ourselves from him, speaking to him neither bad nor good, as the manner of some is, who have the art of concealing their displeasure till they have an opportunity of a full revenge (2 Sa. 13:22); but we must rather give vent to our resentments with the meekness of wisdom, endeavour to convince our brother of the injury, reason the case fairly with him, and so put an end to the disgust conceived: this is the rule our Saviour gives in this case, Lu. 17:3. 2. Therefore rebuke him for his sin against God, because thou lovest him; endeavour to bring him to repentance, that his sin may be pardoned, and he may turn from it, and it may not be suffered to lie upon him. Note, Friendly reproof is a duty we owe to one another, and we ought both to give it and take it in love. Let the righteous smite me, and it shall be a kindness, Ps. 141:5. Faithful and useful are those wounds of a friend, Prov. 27:5, 6. It is here strictly commanded, "Thou shalt in any wise do it, and not omit it under any pretence." Consider, (1.) The guilt we incur by not reproving: it is construed here into a hating of our brother. We are ready to argue thus, "Such a one is a friend I love, therefore I will not make him uneasy by telling him of his faults;" but we should rather say, "therefore I will do him the kindness to tell him of them." Love covers sin from others, but not from the sinner himself. (2.) The mischief we do by not reproving: we suffer sin upon him. Must we help the ass of an enemy that has fallen under his burden, and shall we not help the soul of a friend? Ex. 23:5. And by suffering sin upon him we are in danger of bearing sin for him, as the margin reads it. If we reprove not the unfruitful works of darkness, we have fellowship with them, and become accessaries ex post facto— after the fact, Eph. 5:11. It is thy brother, thy neighbour, that is concerned; and he was a Cain that said, Am I my brother's keeper?

VIII. We are here required to put off all malice, and to put on brotherly love, v. 18. 1. We must be ill-affected to none: Thou shalt not avenge, nor bear any grudge; to the same purport with that v. 17, Thou shalt not hate thy brother in thy heart; for malice is murder begun. If our brother has done us an injury, we must not return it upon him, that is avenging; we must not upon every occasion upbraid him with it, that is bearing a grudge; but we must both forgive it and forget it, for thus we are forgiven of God. It is a most ill-natured thing, and the bane of friendship, to retain the resentment of affronts and injuries, and to let that word devour for ever. 2. We must be well-affected to all: Thou shalt love thy neighbour as thyself. We often wrong ourselves, but we soon forgive ourselves those wrongs, and they do not at all lessen our love to ourselves; and in like manner we should love our neighbour. Our Saviour has made this the second great commandment of the law (Mt. 22:39), and the apostle shows how it is the summary of all the laws of the second table, Rom. 13:9, 10; Gal. 5:14. We must love our neighbour as truly as we love ourselves, and without dissimulation; we must evidence our love to our neighbour in the same way as that by which we evidence our love to ourselves, preventing his hurt, and procuring his good, to the utmost of our power. We must do to our neighbour as we would be done to ourselves (Mt. 7:12), putting our souls into his soul's stead, Job 16:4, 5. Nay, we must in many cases deny ourselves for the good of our neighbour, as Paul, 1 Co. 9:19, etc. Herein the gospel goes beyond even that excellent precept of the law; for Christ, by laying down his life for us, has taught us even to lay down our lives for the brethren, in some cases (1 Jn. 3:16), and so to love our neighbour better than ourselves.[99]

---

[99] Matthew Henry, Matthew Henry's Commentary on the Whole Bible: Complete and Unabridged in One Volume (Peabody: Hendrickson, 1994), 173–174.

~ INDEX ~

Ambrose, 12
Anger, 30, 31
Apostasy, 25
Apostles, 25
Blasphemy, 25
Bunyan, John, 10, 101
Christ
  Falsely accused, 17
Christian
  Children of God, 17, 95
  Discernment ministries, 78
  False, 10
  Forgiven of sin, 99
  Imperfection and sanctification, 84
  Inconsistent conduct, 76, 77
  Justification, 90
  Justified by faith, 90, 99
  New nature, 22
  Self delusion, 22
Clickbait, 82
Complaining spirit, 58

INDEX

Corinthian church, 24, 25
Deception, 44
Discernment, 78, 79, 80, 81, 82, 83, 86
Doctrine
  Weak, 25
Easy-believism, 25
Einstein's mass-energy equivalence, 15
Electronic communications. *See* Internet
Entertainment-crazed society, 71
Ethnicity, 23, 51
Evil
  Inestimable, 16
  Spiritual forces of wickedness, 18, 80
  Two sources, 17
  Underestimation of, 16, 36
Evil speech, 20, 31, 45, 50, 51, 53, 56, 61, 65, 72
Facebook, 28
Faith
  Dead, 59
  Saving, 21
False accusations, 17
False brethren, 59, 84, 85, 86
False prophets, 46
False teaching, 82, 84
False witness, 26, 29, 31, 45, 46, 47, 77
FBI, 28
Feigned Graciousness, 50
Flame-thrower "ministries", 82
Genealogy, 23
God
  Creator of all, 41, 45
  Everlasting retribution, 48
  Fear of, 19
  His supreme authority, 41
  Holiness, 21
  Holy hatred of sin, 45, 46
  Holy Spirit, 22
  Immutable faithfulness, 46
  Lawgiver and Judge, 60, 61, 62, 70
  Love of, 42, 43
  Omniscience, 31, 35
  Patience and mercy, 41
  Will not trifle with sin, 34
  Will of, 37, 64, 84, 111
Google, 28

Gospel, the, 10, 21, 23, 50, 54, 77, 84, 87, 90, 92, 93, 94, 104, 110
Hearing slander, 50
Heart of man
  Continual evil, 32
  Intentions, 32
Hell, 11, 12, 16, 17, 18, 19, 21, 23, 30, 31, 55
  Eternal abode of the damned, 16
Hellish speech, 12, 20, 28, 44, 56, 75
Human heart
  Bearing a grudge, 68
  Hatred, 64
  Repentance, 25, 63, 72, 84, 87, 106, 120
  Seeking to be God's substitute, 62, 70
  Underestimating sin, 35
Humor, 48
Hypocrisy, 11, 57, 58, 59, 60, 70, 77, 84
Idolatry, 46
Infernus, 12
Internet, 4, 10, 12, 16, 19, 24, 25, 28, 37, 50, 60, 64, 71, 73, 76, 77, 82, 83, 85
Jesting, 49
Jesus Christ
  Crucified, 95, 96, 97, 98, 99
  Crucifixion, 22
  Deity, 92, 94
  Eternal life, 21, 23, 93, 98, 99, 104
  Eternality, 94
  Exclusivity of, 23
  Foremost commandment, 42, 68, 71, 78, 84, 86, 87
  Incarnation, 22, 92, 93, 94, 99
  Mediator, 91
  Mocked and reviled, 96
  on Marriage, 40
  Perfect obedience, 92
  Resurrection, 22, 99
  Savior, 23, 64, 66, 84, 95, 97, 98
  Sinless substitute, 22
  The eternal Son of God, 22
  True peace, 24
Jewell, Richard, 27, 28, 29, 76
Judgment
  eternal, 21, 90
  of Christ, 17
lex talionis, 47
LGBT, 39

INDEX

Love
　for the brethren, 17
　Forgiveness, 69
　Patience of, 69
Lying, 17, 19, 45, 46, 47, 48, 49, 50, 77, 113, 116
　Forensic, 46
Malicious witness, 47
Mankind
　Children of wrath, 18
Marketing scams, 12
Materialism, 58
Mockery, 20, 28, 49, 50, 71, 96, 98
Moses, 43, 92, 99, 108
Mythology, 84
New York Times, 28
News Media
　ABC, 28
　Atlanta Journal Constitution, 28
　CNN, 28
Ninth commandment, 29
Noah, 34
non-Christian
　Slave of sin, 23
Perjury, 46
Pornography, 12
Pride, 32, 34, 58, 61, 70
Rebellion, 34, 40, 49, 58, 71

Rebuke, 10, 11, 17, 34, 42, 43, 44, 55, 60, 64, 67, 68, 69, 70, 71, 72, 73, 78, 83, 119, 120
Religionists, 31
Reproof, 11, 44, 66, 67, 71, 72, 73, 81, 82, 102, 120
　Self examination, 70
Resurrection, 22
Rudolph, Eric, 28
Salvation
　Not by works, 22
Satan, 17, 20, 25, 29, 30, 37, 54, 55, 58, 60, 63, 76, 84
　Accuser of the brethren, 12, 30, 61
　co-belligerence, 17, 37, 53, 55, 57, 58, 60, 63
　Devil, 12, 17, 18, 29, 30, 58, 72, 106
　Devil's own children, 17
　Father of lies, 17, 20, 29, 37
　Imitation of, 61, 64
　Murderer, 12, 17, 29, 30
　Self exaltation, 63
Scribes and Pharisees, the, 31

Scripture, 4, 19, 20, 21, 22, 24, 50, 66, 67, 71, 83, 85, 94, 104
  Comprehensible revelation, 66
  Descriptive vs. Prescriptive passages, 49
  Equipping, 66
  Law as a tutor, 90
  Profitable for teaching, 66
  Sword of the Spirit, 80, 83
  Training in righteousness, 66, 67, 71
Selfish divisions, 58
Sin
  Lusts, 18, 58, 113
  Universal reality, 13, 21, 36, 99
Subjectivism, 41, 45
Superficial religiosity, 31
Swearing falsely, 46
The Pilgrim's Progress, 10, 86, 101, 102
The Pilgrim's Progress
  Faithful, 10, 102, 103, 105, 109, 114, 120

Talkative, 10, 11, 86, 102, 103, 105, 107, 108, 109, 113, 114
Tongue
  Talebearer, 42, 68
Tongue, the
  a fire, 11, 16
  Boastful, 22, 36, 79
  Calumniation, 61
  Coarse Jesting, 49
  Complaining, 58, 59
  Deceitful Jesting, 48
  Defiles the entire body, 11, 16
  Destruction of others, 79, 81
  False accusers, 47
  Foolish speech, 49
  Giving of thanks, 24, 49
  Gossip, 48
  Gratuitous sarcasm, 49
  Hate speech, 39, 40, 42, 44
  Lying, 17, 29, 30, 37, 46, 56, 72, 110, 111, 113, 115, 116, 120
  Power of, 19, 51, 75
  Satanic, 29, 53, 58, 60, 62, 63
  Set on fire by hell, 11, 16

INDEX

Slander, 30, 43, 48, 49, 50, 59, 61, 62, 75, 77, 81, 83, 107
Spreading strife, 46
Strife, 47
the very world of iniquity, 11, 16
Unbridled, 58, 63, 77
Whisperer, 50
Twitter, 28
Vengeance, 6, 42, 43, 68, 81, 116, 117
Victimhood, false, 17
Wisdom
  Demonic, 56, 57, 64
  Purity, 56
Witnesses, 47, 95
Wolves in sheep's clothing, 85
Worthless religion, 60

Proverbs 3:5-18:

5 Trust in Jehovah with all thy heart,
And lean not upon thine own understanding:
6 In all thy ways acknowledge him, And he will direct thy paths.
7 Be not wise in thine own eyes; Fear Jehovah, and depart from
evil: 8 It will be health to thy navel, And marrow to thy bones. 9
Honor Jehovah with thy substance, And with the first-fruits of
all thine increase: 10 So shall thy barns be filled with plenty, And
thy vats shall overflow with new wine. 11 My son, despise not
the chastening of Jehovah; Neither be weary of his reproof: 12
For whom Jehovah loveth he reproveth; Even as a father the son
in whom he delighteth. 13 Happy is the man that findeth
wisdom, And the man that getteth understanding. 14 For the
gaining of it is better than the gaining of silver, And the profit
thereof than fine gold. 15 She is more precious than rubies: And
none of the things thou canst desire are to be compared unto
her. 16 Length of days is in her right hand; In her left hand are
riches and honor.17 Her ways are ways
of pleasantness, And all her
paths are peace.
18 She is a
tree of life
to them that
lay hold
upon her:
And happy
is every
one that
retaineth
her.

www.ingramcontent.com/pod-product-compliance
Lightning Source LLC
Chambersburg PA
CBHW020008050426
42450CB00005B/364